D0287949

STEPHENS COLLEGE

DISCARD

LIBRARY

CHRISTIANITY
and the
SCIENTIST

the HADDAM HOUSE *series on*
THE CHRISTIAN IN HIS VOCATION

Edward LeRoy Long, Jr.
SERIES EDITOR

The Christian as a Doctor
James T. Stephens and
Edward LeRoy Long, Jr.

Christianity and the Scientist
Ian G. Barbour

CHRISTIANITY
and the
SCIENTIST

by IAN G. BARBOUR

ASSOCIATION PRESS   NEW YORK

Copyright © 1960 by
National Board of Young Men's Christian Associations

Association Press, 291 Broadway, New York 7, N.Y.

All rights reserved, including the right of reproduction in whole or in part in any form, under the International, Pan-American, and Universal Copyright Conventions.

Library of Congress Catalog Card Number: 60-12715

 72

Printed in the United States of America

Stephens College
Columbia, Missouri

BL
240.2
.B35

to **DEANE**

81750

Recollection of the sometimes bitter struggles between science and religion during the past four or five centuries leads many people to suppose that the life and work of a scientist is a purely secular affair. To be sure, many scientists belong to Christian churches, but their relation to the church is kept in one compartment of their thinking and their relationship to their job is kept in another.

The day is past when natural scientists as a group are predominately opposed to religion, if indeed it ever existed at all. Nevertheless, many scientists are perplexed as to just how the vocation of a scientist has meaning as a Christian calling. Much has been written about science and religion in general, but little has appeared to help scientists find Christian meaning in their jobs as scientists. It is one thing to justify the intellectual validity of the scientific enterprise; it is another to understand that enterprise as a positive avenue of service to God.

The following discussion is an effort to point the ways along which the life of the scientist—in research or teaching, in industrial, collegiate, or governmental service—can be so understood and so conducted as to make it a worthy means of expressing Christian discipleship. There are no spectacular suggestions here, no formulae for putting God into the laboratory, no reliance upon patterns of behavior unacceptable to

7

scientists or unrelated to the task of the scientist understood in its broadest sense. The vocation of the scientist is considered in its widest setting, its moral implications are seriously explored, and its responsibilities to truth and to society are acknowledged—but the task itself is not overhauled.

This is as it should be. To introduce extraneous considerations into the technical work of the scientist would violate the integrity of the profession. To rely upon activities or patterns of behavior outside the daily work of the scientist as means for expressing a Christian response to God's call would be to abandon the conviction of Reformed theology that any useful work done soberly and well can be a valid means of serving God.

The author brings to this inquiry training and experience as a physicist, as well as study in theology. He is listed in *American Men of Science* and has contributed to both scientific and religious journals. In this volume he gives concrete examples of some of the ethical dilemmas scientists have actually faced. He has wisely avoided the claim that there is only one way in which the life of the scientist can be a proper life of devotion to God. The positions he has taken with candor and defended with clarity do not bind the conscience of the reader, but they do challenge the reader to make his own equally clear and equally dedicated responses. It would be unfaithful to both the best in the world of scientific learning and the wisest kind of religious leadership to offer more than these broad clear strokes in the portrayal of what it means in our day to undertake the work of a scientist as a Christian calling.

EDWARD LEROY LONG, JR.
Series Editor

CONTENTS

Chapter 1

INTRODUCTION: THE VOCATION
OF THE SCIENTIST

Among the members of the Royal Society of London in the seventeenth century were many of the founding fathers of modern science. The charter of the Society directs its members to pursue their work *"to the glory of God the Creator and the advantage of the human race."* Can the scientist today share such motives in his work? Of contemporary scientists, 70 per cent believe in the existence of God and 40 per cent are church members.[1] Do such beliefs have any relation to scientific work?

There are of course no specifically Christian laws of science. Religious faith has nothing to say about the valence of oxygen or the mass of the electron. The boiling point of sulfur does not depend on the investigator's philosophy of life. But there are a number of aspects of the vocation of the scientist to which religious perspectives are relevant. Being a Christian geologist does not mean finding oil on church property. It means serving God and man in the daily work of geology. Our task is to analyze what this implies in terms of the practical problems of the job.

Many books have been written about science and religion

in general, dealing with ideas and issues in the abstract. This volume, however, looks at persons and their existential lives. It is concerned with the scientist himself, the man with two areas of loyalty: dedication to science and commitment to God. How do these two loyalties interact? At what points does he confront ethical choices in his job? What are his motives in his work?

To picture the man under consideration we may describe him by his subject, his habitat, and his goal:

His subject: natural science. This inquiry is limited to work in the physical sciences (physics, chemistry, geology, astronomy) and the biological sciences (zoology, botany, agriculture). Medicine, engineering, and the social sciences each raise distinctive issues which are not discussed here. But within each of the natural sciences is a variety of workers: the technician carrying out routine operations, the teacher training a new generation, the research expert making new discoveries or developing industrial applications.

His habitat: industry, government, or education. In industry the scientist finds higher salaries, the satisfaction of seeing practical results, and sometimes better research facilities. In education he finds salaries lower but usually enjoys greater independence; he has more contact with people, and often a chance to combine teaching and research. Government projects are intermediate between industrial and educational jobs in both salary and freedom.

His goal: pure or applied science. Fundamental research, sometimes called pure science, aims at understanding the natural world; it issues in the basic concepts and principles of science. In contrast, applied science is concerned with technological applications which are useful in man's life. It yields new processes, new materials, devices, and machines, primarily under the sponsorship of industry. But there is no sharp line between pure and applied work, and each is dependent on the other.

People choose careers and continue to work in science for many reasons. Often such decisions are less a matter of deliberate choice than of chance and circumstance. A person may have been influenced by family expectations, or the inspiration of a gifted teacher, or a specific job opening. Moreover, scientists seldom talk about their motives; they are likely to insist that the place in which they work is a *LABOR*atory, not a lab*ORATORY*. But whether men talk about them or not, they do have a variety of motivations. For some, income or prestige is a major goal. For scientists, work is seldom, however, simply a means to earn a living. Undoubtedly the desire for recognition, particularly the respect of fellow scientists, is an important stimulus. The symbols of success and some of the temptations of the job will be examined later.

A central motive in any job is the expression of one's *interests* and *abilities*. Most scientists find great enjoyment in their work, whether it is the excitement of a new discovery, the satisfaction of developing an "elegant" theory, building a useful piece of apparatus, or watching a student really grasp the solution to a problem. In such activities there is opportunity for creative self-expression and continued growth. A person is likely to be happier himself and to make his greatest contribution to society if he works in a job which utilizes his natural aptitudes rather than in one for which he has little interest or ability.

The biblical understanding of vocation encourages a person to serve God in whatever useful work he can do best. "Calling" or "vocation" means primarily the call to acknowledge a relationship to God, and to live in responsible obedience to him wherever one is. Hence it also means a call to a particular task, and response to God in one's daily work. The Reformers denied any sharp division between "sacred" and "secular," and rejected the idea that the work of the clergyman is inherently superior to other callings. They emphasized the significance of the layman and the meaningfulness and dignity of labor. A leveling of occupations is reflected in Luther's writing: "Even a small work, even a maid cooking and cleaning, must be praised as a service to God far surpassing the holiness and asceticisms of all monks." Contemporary Protestantism has seen a rebirth of this concern for the role of the layman and the relation of work and faith. Many authors [2] have written of the compartmentalization of life today and the danger when religion is confined within the four walls of the church. Man's response to God takes place within a wider community and is expressed in the life of the world.

There are many ways in which one might try to formulate the various elements in the calling of every man. We will describe it in terms of four aspects: the vocation *to serve human need, to seek truth, to work for a better society, and to worship God.* These responses are interrelated—for example, the pursuit of truth may be a form of both service to man and appreciation of God's creation. In prophetic religion, concern for the need of the neighbor and concern for justice in the social order are seen as precisely the kind of worship most acceptable to God. Though these aspects of a man's calling are interrelated, we shall consider each in turn as it is expressed in the work of the scientist.

The following chapter is an analysis of the vocation to serve human need in relation to applied science. Science has improved health, raised standards of living, and alleviated suffering. If love of neighbor is not a sentimental attitude but actual response to human needs, science can obviously be a potent instrument of good will. But technology has had destructive as well as constructive consequences. To what extent is a scientist responsible for the uses to which his inventions are put?

In Chapter 3 the vocation to seek truth is considered, primarily in terms of fundamental research. Most scientists are driven by intellectual curiosity and the desire to know, as much as by interest in practical applications. A recent survey found "intellectual satisfactions" rated by scientists as the most important source of satisfaction in their work, with "the social value of their work" rated a strong second.[3] What are the strengths and limitations of the pursuit of knowledge, and its relation to religious perspectives?

In Chapter 4 the specific case of the science teacher, with some of his opportunities and problems, is examined. Chapter 5 concerns the unique ways in which the scientist, both as citizen and as specialist, can express the vocation to work for a better society. The final chapter deals with his vocation to worship God, and the impact of technical work on his personal life and religious beliefs.

Other occupations also provide channels for serving human need, seeking truth, working for a better society, and worshiping God. There is urgent need for dedicated and able psychologists, statesmen, and ministers, for example. Men in various jobs can work side by side, each understanding his activity as a particular expression of the same fourfold calling, and each dedicated to making some contribution to their common goal. Our concern here, however, is with the person who does have abilities and interest in science, and these are presupposed in all that follows; for without them a person would neither survive the competition of university training nor contribute significantly through scientific work.

The initial duty in applied science, research, or teaching is to do the job well: to design an airplane wing that will hold under stress, to find a valid equation for chemical equilibrium, or to help students gain sound understanding of metabolism. There are no Christian laws of science, and there are of course many outstanding scientists who have no

interest in religion. So we must ask: What are the particular
motives of the Christian in each aspect of scientific work?
At what points might his religious faith make a difference?
What problems arise because of his loyalty both to the scientific enterprise and to God?

Chapter 2

APPLIED SCIENCE AND HUMAN WELFARE

A CHEMIST IS WORKING FOR A COMPANY WHICH POURS waste products into a stream, polluting it in a way that, for a reasonable cost, could be avoided. In recommending policy at such a point, is this man's first duty to his employer or to the public? Eighteen top German physicists, including four Nobel prize winners, stated in 1957 that they would not work on projects having any connection with nuclear weapons. Were they right in assuming that the scientist has some responsibility for the uses to which his discoveries are put? This chapter deals with the moral decisions involved in expressing through applied science the Christian vocation to serve human need.

A. SCIENCE: CREATOR AND DESTROYER

In the last hundred years, science has had an impact on almost every aspect of life in the West. Men have been released from backbreaking labor, living standards have risen, and leisure has increased. New drugs, cures of formerly fatal diseases, and improvement of health standards have more than doubled the average life span in the last century. New products, processes, and machines surround us on every hand, from our electrified homes to our industrialized cities. A trip from New York to San Francisco, which required four months in 1860, takes four hours by jet plane.

With the release of men from deadening drudgery and toil, new possibilities of cultural growth and the use of man's varied capacities have emerged. Education and an enriched intellectual life have been more widespread, encouraged by the demands of an industrial civilization for skilled workers. For the first time in history, abundance is possible for every nation—not, as in the past, at the expense of others, but through a nation's own scientific development. The ancient dream of a society free from famine, disease, poverty, and despair is beginning to be fulfilled by the applications of science.

The need for scientific progress is illustrated by the situation faced today in underdeveloped countries. About half of the babies born in most parts of Africa and Asia die in childhood. Those who survive face a life of squalor and misery. In India, for example, the average life expectancy is 30½ years, compared to 68½ years in the United States; the average annual income is less than $40, compared to $1,469 in the U.S. Energy utilized annually per capita, which is a rough index of living standard, is in some countries equivalent to .02 tons of coal, compared to 8 tons, or 400 times as much, in the U.S. Two thirds of the world usually goes to bed hungry at night. A correspondent reports:

> In Persia I talked with a peasant who has seen a can of our dog food. He said that if he could get such a can once a week for his family he would be happy. He might be willing to die to realize his ambition to lead the life of an American dog.[1]

Clearly one of the justifications of science is its contribution to human welfare. Science can be an instrument of

good will, extending the reach of the good Samaritan's hand.
Central in Christian ethics is love of neighbor, which means
concrete action to meet his needs. Biblical religion is not primarily otherworldly, nor is it interested only in "π in the
sky by and by." It finds crucial meaning in this world, for
example in how one treats other people. Jesus was concerned
about men's bodies as well as their minds. "I was sick and
you visited me" (Matthew 25:36). "If your enemy is hungry,
feed him" (Romans 12:20). Thus Kirtley Mather, the Harvard geologist, can say:

> Science is obviously in the service of religion. One of the
> keynotes of every great religion is expressed in the desire
> that the sick should be made well, blind eyes opened,
> unfortunate economic situations set aright, that persons
> in positions which give them no opportunity to display
> their own real worth should be given that opportunity. . . .
> Is it not obvious that religion has profited greatly by the
> knowledge which science gives along such practical lines
> as these? [2]

The chief justification for any work is that it meets genuine
human needs. Some commentators, however, feel that this
should not be the main Christian motive in science because
it would "reduce Christianity to an ethical system." William
Pollard, executive director of the Oak Ridge Institute for
Nuclear Studies, argues that ethics is not the main message
of Christianity, and that humanitarian goals for science are
held also by agnostics having secular objectives.[3] However,
concern for others is an essential part of the Christian faith,
even though religion is more than ethics alone. And Western
culture has been so influenced by the biblical tradition that
"humanitarianism" in any form may owe a greater debt to
Christianity than it recognizes. Surely scientists may legiti-

mately see their work as a Christian response to human needs.

But if science can be justified by its constructive results, what can be said of its destructive consequences? The possibilities for both good and evil uses of new discoveries have been repeatedly illustrated in the history of science. Leonardo da Vinci suppressed his plans for a submarine: "This I do not divulge on account of the evil nature of men who would practice assassinations at the bottom of the sea by breaking ships in their lowest parts and sinking them." Napier refused to publish the ingredients of an explosive. Alfred Nobel thought that in inventing dynamite he had made a weapon so powerful that war would be impossible; disillusioned, he gave part of the fortune he made from it to establish the Nobel Peace Prize. Thus the problem of the destructive power unlocked by science is no new one, though it has achieved a new magnitude in our time.

The scientists working on the atomic bomb recognized at an early stage some of the implications of their work. The Franck report was written at the Chicago project in June, 1945, two months before Hiroshima:

> If the United States were to be the first to release this new means of indiscriminate destruction upon mankind, she would sacrifice public support throughout the world, precipitate the race for armaments, and prejudice the possibility of reaching an international agreement on the future control of such weapons. Much more favorable conditions for the eventual achievement of such an agreement could be created if nuclear bombs were first revealed to the world by a demonstration in an appropriately selected uninhabited area.[4]

In contrast to the Franck report, the decision to drop the bomb on civilian populations was governed mainly by immediate military considerations. "Unconditional surrender" had become an end in itself, at the expense of clarity about the political goals for which we were fighting. The U.S. did not even try to exploit by diplomacy the intercepted cables which were decoded during July, indicating that Japan was trying through Russian intermediaries to negotiate a surrender on all our terms except the retention of the Emperor—which, after using the bomb, we were to allow anyway. Louis Morton, deputy chief historian of the Army, summarizes the situation in July:

> Thus the Japanese Government had by then accepted defeat and was seeking desperately for a way out; but it was not willing even at this late date to surrender unconditionally, and would accept no terms that did not include the preservation of the imperial system.[5]

Michael Armine's recent reappraisal, *The Great Decision,* states:

> Grew, Stimson, McCloy, and many men in uniform who were familiar with Asia, such as Zacharias [the man in charge of psychological-warfare broadcasts to Japan], came to feel that a grave error of our surrender policy was in not negotiating about the Emperor and conditional surrender sooner that we did.[6]

It is in terms of such policy questions that one must evaluate the fact that mankind's first use of atomic energy took from two cities 120,000 lives.

The continuing sense of social concern among the atomic scientists was a striking feature of the postwar years. J. R. Oppenheimer, who directed the Los Alamos project, wrote afterward:

> The experience of the war has left us with a legacy of concern. Nowhere is this troubled sense of responsi-

bility more acute ... than among those who participated in the development of atomic energy for military
purposes. ... In some sort of crude sense, which no
vulgarity, no humor, no overstatement can quite extin-
guish, the physicists have known sin; and this is a
knowledge that they cannot lose.[7]

The *Bulletin of the Atomic Scientists* was launched, and has
continued to deal responsibly and influentially with social and
political implications of science. Scientists campaigned suc-
cessfully for civilian rather than military administration of
atomic energy. They continued to warn the public of the
destructive power of atomic weapons and the urgent need for
international controls. More recently, the American Association for the Advancement of Science (AAAS) established a
Committee on the Social Aspects of Science, whose 1956
report spoke of "the pressing need that scientists concern
themselves with social action" and urged scientific organizations to abandon their traditional isolation from public
problems.

The effects of science on society present a mixed record
of good and evil. The automobile brings mobility to the
average man, but U.S. traffic deaths in the last decade ex-
ceeded our fatalities in World War II. TV and radio provide
new channels for the communication of ideas, but make it
easier for dictators to control nations, or for trivial entertain-
ment to mold the mass mind. Technical advances produce
new products but make possible new centralizations of political power in the police state, and new concentrations of
economic power in industry. These destructive powers, especially in warfare, have led some authors, e.g., Aldous Huxley,
to call for a moratorium on science. Yet without the con-
tinuance of the work of the scientist millions of people would
suffer or die of hunger and disease in a few years. Further,

our consciousness of knowledge already gained cannot be erased, nor could man's desire for knowledge be thwarted except at the price of his freedom. Any instrument of good can be misused. A total pessimist about human nature might avoid scientific activity; a total optimist might have no cause for concern about its consequences. But a person who sees in man potentialities for both good and evil will combine scientific work with the attempt to exert his influence toward its beneficial use.

B. THE SOCIAL RESPONSIBILITY OF THE SCIENTIST

To what extent is the scientist responsible for the uses to which his work is put? The problem arises not only in the dramatic case of atomic energy but in thousands of lesser cases in which an application has significant consequences for society. P. W. Bridgman, Harvard's Nobel-prize physicist, has argued that in most occupations individual blame does not extend to all results of an act: the miner of iron ore is not expected to think about all the uses of iron.

> For if I personally had to see to it that only beneficent uses were made of my discoveries, I should have to spend my life oscillating between some kind of a forecasting bureau, to find what might be the uses made of my discoveries, and lobbying in Washington to procure the passage of special legislation to control the uses. In neither of these activities do I have any competence.[8]

He sees the concern of the atomic scientists as misguided, "a youthful philosophy, enthusiastic, idealistic, and colored by eagerness for self-sacrifice." "If anybody should feel guilty, it's God, who put the facts there." He also feels that it is unfair for the public to "impose" responsibility on scientists, which is to "exact disproportionate service from one group because of their special ability." Other writers have said that the scientist must be free to search for the truth without having to consider the consequences. The outcomes of research, they argue, are unpredictable; moreover, it is the job of society, not of the individual, to make such decisions. I. I. Rabi adds: "Scientists who dabble in politics usually make fools out of themselves."

This commonly held position seems to the author to be inadequate in the case of applied science, where effects can usually be foreseen to some extent. Even in pure research a person often has a general idea of the sort of results that are likely to follow, and the motives of the project's sponsor indicate the type of outcome for which he hopes. Furthermore, those who say they disavow all accountability except to the pursuit of truth would probably draw the line at some point. Who would condone Nazi experimentation on human guinea pigs, even though the data added to knowledge? Or again, would a biochemist, asked by a crime syndicate to develop a poison which would be undetectable at autopsy, be able to ignore the consequences of such a discovery? To most scientists, research on germ warfare is abhorrent. The question, then, is not whether to draw a line, but at what point to draw it.

The attempt to delegate all responsibility to society must also be scrutinized. The Nuremberg trials did not exonerate German scientists of individual answerability for their work, even though they were acting on orders. Even in a democracy, it is a dubious interpretation which says that the individual must always conform to the opinion of the majority. The essence of democracy is not rule by majority but rather government by discussion, including the right of the minority to be heard. To be a free man means to take responsibility for one's own actions. For the Christian in particular, absolute allegiance to nation or group can never come before obedience to God as he understands it. In an age of conformity the significance of individual conscience must not be lost, nor the integrity of the man who says with Luther: "Here I stand; I can do no other."

A further objection may be raised concerning Bridgman's view of the nature of responsibility. Moral responsibility is not primarily a burden "imposed" on the individual by society, but an opportunity for constructive action, voluntarily acknowledged. The word responsibility comes from the verb "to respond" and represents a person's response to his total situation. The main question is not whether society blames me for what I do, but whether I can find ways of making a maximum positive contribution, or do anything to prevent destructive results. Eugene Rabinowitch comments on Bridgman's article: "Does he expect to find satisfaction, as he contemplates the radioactive ruins of Harvard Yard, in the thought that he, at least, had resisted all attempts to saddle him with responsibility that was not his?" The opportunity of the scientist may be greater than that of the average citizen with respect to some issues because his technical knowledge gives him greater understanding and appreciation of them, and because he has considerable influence in contemporary life. And if there are some scientific geniuses who can give the greatest service to society by giving attention only to their work, they should do even this as an expression of, not an escape from, responsibility. Actually Bridgman himself has been actively involved as a citizen in a number of public issues; these criticisms are directed not at his own practice, but at the common viewpoint, of which he has been a forceful spokesman, disavowing concern for the uses of a scientist's work.

Many scientists are simply indifferent to the social implications of their job. For every one who consciously disclaims accountability for his work, there are dozens who do so by default because of:

1. *Absorption in technical work.* Concern for human welfare will play little or no role for the man whose only motivations are curiosity and technical interest. Research is a time-consuming process and can easily absorb a man's entire attention. Some men were attracted to the H-bomb project only because it was exciting and they were eager to take part in a brilliant scientific achievement. The British major in *The Bridge on the River Kwai* [9] was motivated by professional pride in "doing a good job" without asking about the purposes it served. He built a superb bridge and kept the morale of his men on a high level, but realized too late that his technical success had aided his country's enemy.

2. *Bureaucratic organization.* Laboratories in both industry and government are components of power-hierarchies in which most individuals have little control over policy. Such a situation discourages responsible participation in decision-making. Specialization often isolates one part of a project from other parts of the same operation. When men work in teams, no individual feels responsible for decisions; even the project director is carrying out directives. A scientist easily becomes what Whyte calls "the Organization Man," accommodating to the expectations of others concerning his work role. It is easier to "fit in" and "go along," in unquestioning loyalty to the group, than to raise questions about what the organization is doing.

3. *Caution about value-judgments.* Some scientists try to avoid social or moral questions. They feel that their training has encouraged them to be detached and impersonal, wary of individual preferences. But the avoidance of personal commitment may only encourage the exploitation of one's

talents by someone else—politician, industrialist, or the state. And decision can not be so easily avoided: silence may mean consent to the *status quo,* and not to act is often itself a decision. More often the scientist, because of specialized training and a busy schedule, is simply ignorant of the wider issues on which his work touches.

4. *Faith in automatic progress.* The spectacular development of early science gave rise to the eighteenth-century optimism that increase of knowledge would lead inevitably to happiness and virtue. In the nineteenth century, evolution was often interpreted as a guarantee of universal advance. Some scientists continue the assumption of the rationality and goodness of man; with such confidence in progress one does not need to be concerned about the uses that will be made of one's work, since it is assumed that the end result of all discovery is beneficial. But every new advance brings its new problems and temptations, as well as benefits. Technical development is cumulative, but moral progress is more precarious, as the efficiency of the Buchenwald extermination camps reminds us.

In contrast to those who either consciously disavow or unconsciously neglect the implications of their work, some authors insist that every individual is answerable for the consequences of his research. Norbert Wiener, Massachusetts Institute of Technology mathematician, withheld some of his results and said: "I do not expect to publish any future work of mine which may do damage in the hands of irresponsible militarists." [10] The Society for Social Responsibility in Science (SSRS) has as its purpose "to foster throughout the world a functioning cooperative tradition of personal moral responsibility for the consequences for humanity of professional activity, with emphasis on constructive alternatives to militarism." Among its members have been Nobellaureates Einstein, Pauli, Born, and Yukawa. Several recent books, e.g., Jungk's *Brighter Than a Thousand Suns*, take this viewpoint in blaming physicists for co-operating in work on the atomic bomb.

Even with respect to applied science, this position perhaps tends to overemphasize individual action, which the position discussed earlier underemphasizes. Since any knowledge may be misused, all technical work involves the acceptance of an element of risk. This risk must be taken if our concern is the maximum probable human benefit rather than the certainty of keeping our own consciences spotless. Perhaps it should be said that the scientist is partially responsible for the probable uses of his work, though not for all its conceivable ramifications. The SSRS position also seems to put disproportionate stress on individual witness, whereas Bridgman's viewpoint went too far in the opposite direction of relegating decisions to others. Since many of the crucial decisions today are made by groups, attention must be given to the scientist's participation in the broader processes of public discussion. To such discussion he can contribute both his technical knowledge and his moral convictions, without claiming unwarranted authority in fields in which he is not an expert. This middle position has been taken by the *Bulletin of the Atomic Scientists* and the Federation of Atomic Scientists, who have operated effectively through channels of communication, education, and political action. *Bulletin* editorials have criticized the tendency of scientists to become "morally irresponsible stooges in a science factory"; and yet they have recognized that in pure research and even in some applied fields it is impossible to predict all uses of new discoveries, much less what their wider effects will be.

If the scientist thus has some responsibility for the outcomes of his work, he will inevitably be involved in moral decisions. What light does religious faith shed on such choices? Christian ethics stresses several criteria: (*a*) *The centrality of love.* By parable, teaching, and example, the New Testament speaks repeatedly of forgiveness and compassion, which require sensitivity, concern, and willingness to act to meet human needs. In terms of the situation between persons, love means reconciliation and the restoration of community. (*b*) *The value of the individual.* Because each person is of value in the sight of God, human personality is sacred, an end and never a means. Response to the individual in need is an expression of worship; it is service to God as well as to man. The goal of action is to give each person the best possible chance to live as God means him to live. (*c*) *Justice as the social expression of love.* Justice is not opposed to love, but is precisely the form which love must take toward groups. Since it is impossible to express love personally toward large numbers of people, it must be embodied in institutional structures which make possible the fulfillment of persons.

We need to go a step further to consider the basis and motivation of such attitudes for the Christian. Concern for others is part of a person's response of gratitude to God. "We love, because he first loved us" (1 John 4:19). The nature of God is thus the basis of ethics: "God is love, and he who abides in love abides in God" (vs. 16). The experience of God's acceptance can free us from the anxieties and insecurities which make us self-defensive; it can enable us to forget about ourselves for a while. This is an ethic of liberty rather than law. What Christ brought to man was not a new code-book of detailed regulations, but a new orientation and attitude from which new modes of action flow.

According to this understanding, the scientist should not expect to find in Christianity a detailed code telling him what to do. He must decide for himself, in the light of all the information he can obtain about the scientific aspects of a concrete situation, plus his understanding of the nature of God and man, and of love and justice. He decides as a whole man, and not first as a technician and then as a Christian. Thus *"responsibility" means "response"*—to the total situation, which includes God, man, and technical data.

One additional factor will influence this response, namely, his attitude toward involvement in the evil of the world. The ethical perfectionist will try to avoid any compromise, for he understands Christian ethics to consist of a set of absolute injunctions. He may resign from his laboratory rather than take part in work which might have harmful consequences. The perspective we have been outlining, however, holds that even though man must strive against corporate evil, he is inescapably implicated in it—for example, in injustices and exploitations by his nation, industry, or group. Practical choices are often ethically ambiguous rather than black and white. A person could try to keep "pure and unspotted" only by withdrawing to a hermitage—though to some people withdrawal to the laboratory gives an illusion of non-involvement. We must aim, then, for whatever social gains can be achieved —even at the price of limited compromise, and always with the risk that some evil may result along with the expected good. The goal is for science as an instrument of love and justice to make the maximum contribution to human welfare.

C. Moral Decisions on the Job

The vocation to serve human need thus requires moral decisions in scientific work. The approach outlined above does not permit the prescription of any simple "Christian answer" to ethical dilemmas. But examples can be given of concrete situations which scientists have faced, and of some of the factors which might be significant from a Christian perspective. The first major choice is the decision among the jobs for which one is qualified. Even though purely accidental factors, such as special preparation or chance openings, may limit the possibilities, there is always some choice of employer and type of work when it comes to selecting a position. Once on a job, many men feel "trapped" in that situation, but there is actually considerable job mobility in science.

Recently a chemist working for a food company turned down an offer from a liquor corporation at twice his current salary because he said that he wanted "to be able at retirement to look back on a useful life." An electrical engineer accepted a job working on a rural electrification project in India, rather than a secure position in an American company. Compare the words of a young physics Ph.D. who had just accepted a job at Los Alamos, the H-bomb center: "I don't believe that what the world needs most is bigger and better bombs. But the job pays well and there is a fine new housing development." Was he not in effect selling his life to the highest bidder? Another man went to Los Alamos because of technical scientific interest in what he thought of as exciting pure research with excellent equipment. Since all work there was at the time "classified," was he not closing his eyes to the main purpose of the project? Note that we are not criticizing those who participated in this project with sincere conviction of its social value, but only those who violated their own personal integrity or ignored the implications of their research. (The problem of national policy and nuclear warfare is discussed later.)

Choice of employment, particularly rejection of work on purely military projects, has been the chief concern of the Society for Social Responsibility in Science. Its dominantly pacifist position forces on it the character of a protest movement, encouraging individual action in withdrawing from "destructive work"; but it has given some attention to constructive alternatives, such as research in agriculture and small industries or technical assistance openings in under-developed countries. A number of outstanding scientists, including the Russian physicist Kapitsa who was for years kept under house arrest by Stalin, have refused to work on anything connected with atomic weapons. A source of current concern is research on germ warfare, which has been the subject of a recent public-relations campaign by the Army. The International Microbiological Congress has passed an unequivocal resolution condemning preparations for bacteriological warfare as unethical. In the light of man's unrelenting attack on disease, some biologists believe that development of deadly germs is a betrayal of the human race as well as of the ideals of science; one-hundredth of an ounce of botulism toxin could kill a million people, and its production seems to further neither scientific knowledge nor any peacetime applications. Whether one approves or disapproves of such research, its implications for mankind cannot be ignored. In choosing employment the Christian must examine the purposes toward which his labors contribute.

Once a job has been selected, other areas of decision must be faced in the course of work. In applied science it is frequently necessary to consider human as well as technical factors—for example, in locating a bridge or highway, or in recommending agricultural methods. Another common problem is the conflict between obligations to employer and to society. Some scientists work for industries which exploit and waste natural resources with little concern for the public. Another situation of tension between the welfare of the consumer and the profits of the employer is the restraint of improvements in a product. There have been many cases in the courts (e.g., improvements in telephones, tires, fluorescent lamps, flashlight bulbs) in which changes that would have greatly lengthened the life or quality of an article were withheld to promote replacement sales.[11] Often patents have been taken out on superior inventions but not used, so that the improvements were completely suppressed and an outmoded product continued. In many European countries, by contrast, a company that does not itself make use of a patent for three years must negotiate license agreements with other companies wishing to use it. Scientists increasingly have a role in policy decisions concerning such questions in both industry and government.

The scientist today is offered various inducements to bestow his benediction on all sorts of products and enterprises, from new tooth pastes to new ways of finding peace of mind. His participation in false or dubious claims contributes to the exploitation of the public. A geologist told the author that he was once instructed "to produce evidence," where there was none, to support a lawsuit concerning the location of a railroad line. In another instance a man was told to "prove" the superiority of the company's material for window frames, though another material was clearly better.

Peculiar temptations are also present in government contracts with industry, since the public which may be defrauded seems so remotely affected. One man working in an industrial laboratory, with half his salary paid by the government, was given his instructions beforehand: "Any discoveries you make which have any scientific or commercial value, and any work you do which is at all profitable, is to appear on the books as having been done on 'company time'; the rest is the government's half of your time. All reports to the government are to be vague and non-committal so as to disclose as little as possible." Desire for prestige and credit may also jeopardize the public interest; one U.S. missile group kept secret from rival groups the transmitter frequency of a satellite about to be orbited.

Another variety of conflict of interests was illustrated in the "Astin affair," in which the director of the National Bureau of Standards was fired because of reactions to a NBS report which found the AD-X2 battery additive "without merit." Scientists all over America protested the dismissal and the pressures exerted against the laboratory's objectivity. The Jeffries Committee evaluated all the evidence from various laboratories and vindicated the Bureau's findings, and Astin was finally reinstated. Clifford Grobstein comments: "A bill of goods, based on too few facts too carelessly evaluated, was sold to a cabinet officer and a congressional committee, and between them they almost wrecked a major scientific laboratory." [12]

The scientist today often becomes the servant of business interests rather than of the pursuit of truth or the welfare of society. A man in industrial research summarized the pressure he felt thus: "It's made clear very soon that neither science nor a good product is the goal; making bucks for the company is the big thing." The Christian perspective on such situations is surely neither unquestioning co-operation nor perfectionistic condemnation. Legitimate economic interests and the realities of power structures can be acknowledged. Yet the person attempting to relate his activities to human welfare must also keep in mind the interests of the consumer and public, both in his own decisions, his participation in policy decisions, and if necessary in his protest against directives he feels to be harmful.

Because ethical choices affecting other people do arise frequently in science, a number of authors have called for an extension of the Hippocratic Oath which for centuries has been associated with medicine. The scientist, like the doctor, has power over the life and well-being of man, and so, it is argued, the public is particularly vulnerable to his code of ethics. There has been recent discussion of the value to science itself, as well as to society, of having a more clearly defined code of professional ethics. The ethics of authorship, obligation to cite prior work, and problems of multiple authorship have been analyzed in an article in *Science*.[13] Others have been concerned about the humane treatment of animals, which are crucial in experimental biology and pharmacology. A biologist reports seeing an extremely painful technique, which most groups use only with full anesthesia, applied by other groups to domestic animals in full consciousness, with no justification except laziness. He commends the British practice of issuing licenses to experimenters subject to specified conditions.[14]

The new field of "operations research," in which scientists have been prominent, appears to escape moral decisions. Its objective is the scientific determination of the most efficient method of achieving a particular goal, e.g., increased output of a factory, maximum military damage in an attack, optimum man-power distribution for a turnpike tollgate staff. But value-judgments have already entered in selecting the goals, in assessment of results, and in choosing the assumptions and criteria in terms of which the "best" procedure is calculated. In the absence of conscious decision these values are taken from cultural presuppositions and assumed to be "obviously desirable."

Another channel of action for the scientist is participation in public decisions relating to his work. It must be granted that in many cases the results of research are unpredictable, and hence it is only through corporate processes that they can be controlled. In Chapter 5 some opportunities of working for a better society are considered, as well as the dangers of naïveté, oversimplification, and unwarranted extension of his authoritative role when a person speaks outside his field of technical competence. But the scientist does have a duty to

inform the public and its leaders about his results and their
implications, and to warn of its dangers. Because of the gap
between the expert and the layman, the interpretation of discoveries to the public is essential for intelligent democratic
decisions. This educational task might take place through in-
terviewing the press, writing letters-to-the-editor, drafting
petitions, giving talks to local groups, or writing semipopular
accounts.

The ethical evaluation of a decision can be made only
within a context which includes social as well as technical
aspects. The moral element is not an extraneous factor but
consists in the relation of the scientific data to human welfare.
An interesting example of the way a man's role "as a person"
includes his role "as a scientist" is provided by the famed
Oppenheimer case. Withdrawal of his security clearance in
1954 involved two main accusations. The first charge was association with Communists in the thirties and subsequent in-
discretions such as his attempt to protect his friend Chevalier.
This charge was prominent in the Atomic Energy Commission's statements and decision, but was given little weight by
the Personnel Security Board (the Gray Board), which after
extensive hearings found "no indication of disloyalty . . . and
eloquent and convincing testimony to his deep devotion to
his country" and "a high degree of discretion reflecting an
unusual ability to keep to himself vital secrets." [15] The second charge, which was the major one in the Gray Board's
report, was that in 1949 he had "failed to display the requi-
site enthusiasm about building the hydrogen bomb." After
the decision was made by the President, he co-operated completely in its execution; but it was held against him that *before*
the decision was made he opposed the development of the
H-bomb on both technical and moral grounds.

The report did not distinguish clearly at this point between *disloyalty* to the nation and honest *dissent* from prevailing opinion as to the best course of action. Oppenheimer felt in 1949, along with many scientists—including all but one of the AEC General Advisory Committee—that it was a dubious gamble to divert major resources into investigation of thermonuclear reactions which might never work. In the hearings [16] Oppenheimer was criticized for "more conservatism than the Air Force would have liked" in being concerned about defensive weapons, and for "interest in the internationalizing of atomic energy" (although the President had appointed him as scientific adviser to Baruch in the United Nations Commission on international controls). It is not surprising that there were a number of people who wished to silence a dissenting voice, and who wanted to claim that scientific and military questions can be kept separate from political and moral ones.

A government agency of course has the right to select its advisers. Oppenheimer's appointment to the AEC Advisory Committee was due to expire the following month and could simply have been allowed to lapse. Instead, disagreement about a particular policy became the main ground for pronouncing him a "security risk" in the Gray Board report. Commissioner Murray filed a separate statement in the AEC decision, which reads in part:

> Even though Dr. Oppenheimer is not an expert on morality, he was quite right in advancing moral reasons for his attitude to the hydrogen bomb program. The scientist is a man before he is a technician. Like every man, he ought to be alert to the moral issues that arise in the course of his work. This alertness is part of his general human civic responsibilities which go beyond his responsibilities as a scientist. When he has moral doubts, he has a right to voice them. Furthermore, it must be

firmly maintained as a principle both of justice and of religious freedom that opposition to governmental policies, based on sincerely held moral opinions, need not make a man a security risk.[17]

The case, though admittedly a very complex one, caused widespread concern among scientists. Theodore White summarizes their reaction:

> The issue, despite the attendant legalism, was whether within the councils of national debate a scientist should be allowed to express an opinion beyond the technique of invention and gadgetry. It was not, as they see it, whether Oppenheimer was right or wrong; but whether in the search for policy a scientist could permit himself the indispensable luxury of offering advice and opinion without exposure to retaliation and charge of crime if the decision went otherwise.[18]

The Oppenheimer case and the earlier example of the decision to use the A-bomb illustrate the intertwining of scientific, political, and ethical questions.

An individual makes moral decisions as a total person, taking all relevant factors into account. Although in general the applied scientist's work clearly contributes to human welfare, there are many concrete choices which he faces in the course of his job. Obviously a non-Christian may have a sense of social responsibility; and for the Christian there is no "easy answer" which can be prescribed for such decisions. But religious faith can increase a person's sensitivity to the ethical dimensions of alternative actions and the implications of his work. It can keep before him every man's vocation to serve human need creatively through his job. And the scientist who sees his life in relation to God and man may perhaps have the courage and the integrity to act in accordance with his convictions.

Chapter *3*

SCIENTIFIC RESEARCH AND THE
PURSUIT OF TRUTH

AN ASTRONOMER IS INVESTIGATING THE SPECTRUM OF LIGHT from a galaxy a million light-years away. Of what value is work of this sort which seems to have no practical use? A biologist has devoted ten years to studying the life-history of a species of spider. For the Christian layman, what can be the motives of such fundamental research? "Pure science" is justified by the applications to which it may eventually lead in unexpected ways, but it is also valuable as part of man's quest for knowledge. In a culture interested in utilitarian results, the importance of the search for understanding in itself must be reaffirmed. The Christian is called not only to serve human need but to seek truth.

A. VALUES IN THE QUEST FOR KNOWLEDGE

The "will to know" is one of man's most characteristic drives. The challenge of the unknown has always attracted men to the exciting adventure of investigation. Curiosity and the desire to understand the universe are the main motivations of many scientists. For every person who wins a Nobel prize for

39

a major discovery, thousands of others find satisfaction in making small contributions to knowledge. Even a science course can convey this sense of intellectual adventure if it stresses the fascinating account of past exploration and encourages the student's own developing insight rather than mere memorization of formulae.

Intellectual achievement is itself one of the finest fruits of human culture. Science represents both a method of understanding the universe and a form of the life of the mind. Newton's three laws were an amazing accomplishment, describing all motions—whether of a tennis ball or of a distant planet. A system of concepts, such as the equations of thermodynamics, is a complex theoretical and experimental structure to which many individuals contributed. Out of apparently unrelated phenomena new patterns emerged; order appeared in what had looked like chaos. There is beauty and simplicity in the laws of nature, and an aesthetic element in the response of the scientist. Poincaré wrote:

> The scientist does not study nature because it is useful; he studies it because he delights in it . . . because it is beautiful. I mean that profounder beauty which comes from the harmonious order of the parts.[1]

Human creativity is prominent in all scientific discovery. Theories require the invention of mental "constructs" in terms of which the data can be understood and organized. Notable advances have usually required new "models" and conceptual schemes, fresh ways of looking at the data, or novel ideas for the design of apparatus. Here imagination and originality are required, and the work of the scientist has much in common with that of the artist. Subsequent appreciation of a scientific theory, like enjoyment of a work of art, requires what J. Bronowski[2] calls "a re-enactment of the original creative moment." Science may well be called "one of the humanities," a product of man's creative spirit.

Truth, beauty, and goodness are all significant values in the life of man. Perhaps in any given enterprise all three should be kept in mind, but one of them is usually predominant. Scientific research is not to be condemned because its particular contribution to the total picture is primarily in the area of truth rather than beauty or goodness. The act of understanding, like artistic activity, is desirable as one part of "the good life," and one aspect of what it means to be truly human. Science has been an emancipator, liberating men from ignorance, fear, and superstition. Furthering knowledge is thus in itself a form of serving human welfare, quite apart from any practical applications.

Moreover, scientific activity requires of its members a number of important ethical attitudes. These values are implicit presuppositions, which only after reflection become conscious ideals:

Rationality and honesty. Deductive and inductive reasoning in relation to experimentation are the essence of scientific thought. Reason enters all phases of work: patient inquiry, critical analysis, mathematical logic, inference and prediction, design of fruitful experiments. Intellectual integrity is necessitated by the character of science itself, for one cannot deceive nature. But this is also a requirement of research as a communal process. Violations of truthfulness are regarded with seriousness, for an individual takes responsibility for the validity of what he publishes and must in turn assume the integrity of the work of others.

Universality and co-operation. Science is international; each man builds on the work of men from many countries and ages. The International Geophysical Year only organized more effectively in a few fields the interaction which has always taken place between nations. Technical talent does not follow lines of race, color, or creed; work is judged by its inherent value, so that mutual respect and democratic relationships are encouraged. Collaboration and teamwork are often essential in research. All contributions to knowledge are common property; thus "private property rights" are minimized, and industrial or government secrecy is accepted only with great reluctance. As each man uses the previous knowledge which the community has lent him, so he is under obligation to publish new data for the use of those who follow him.

Disinterestedness and open-mindedness. The dispassionate requirements of the evidence, not personal preference, provide the criteria for evaluating theories. Private profit and self-interest are seldom the controlling motives of men of science. Tentativeness, suspended judgment, self-criticism, and tolerance of divergent ideas are among the desirable attitudes. To be sure, vehemence of conviction and pride of authorship are as common here as among other creative workers, but the norms of the scientific community minimize the effects of emotional attachment to one's own viewpoint.

Freedom. Science develops most fruitfully when there is freedom of inquiry, thought, and discussion, and the liberty to follow the truth wherever it leads. Publications are subject to open scrutiny and evaluation, tested by criticism and discussion in which the right of dissent is maintained.

The further question arises as to whether these ethical attitudes which are necessary in scientific work can be extended from science to other areas of man's life. A number of authors suggest that the scientist's greatest contribution to civilization is to encourage the widespread adoption of such values. Bronowski urges that scientific attitudes become the ethics of modern man:

> Science has humanized our values. Men have asked for freedom, justice, and respect precisely as the scientific spirit has spread among them.... It is the scientist's duty to teach the implications and values in his work.[3]

Science has indeed been an influence against authoritarianism, dogmatism, and intolerance, and has encouraged freedom of inquiry in general. The scientist can continue to uphold the desirability of experimental attitudes and critical thought in any area of life. His belief in universality and in co-operation across national barriers is a significant example to a divided world; some writers believe this internationalism could be a major force for world peace.

But the proposal to derive ethics completely from science seems to this author to entail several difficulties. It appears to attribute desirable changes in social philosophy in the past too exclusively to the influence of science. Moreover, the scientific enterprise itself is not self-sufficient, but is to some extent dependent on society for the creation and defense of these values. A. D. Ritchie has written:

> These moral qualities are preconditions for the pursuit of science, not products of science except incidentally. ... Belief in free discussion, tolerance, and equal treatment of others, all spring from respect for persons and cannot exist without that respect.... Respect for truth and respect for persons as part of the general social tradition are needed for science to survive.[4]

To be sure, the scientific community always has considerable autonomy, determining its own criteria and the standards it believes to be essential for its work. Yet the traditions of science embody unconscious premises which over a period of time are in two-way interaction with the premises of cultural traditions and institutions. Michael Polanyi [5] suggests, for example, that loyalty to truth presupposes that there is such a thing as truth and that there is an obligation to seek it. This has, in turn, other consequences: freedom, tolerance, and fairness are necessary if we recognize that there is a common truth to which both sides of a dispute are loyal. This dedication to truth cannot simply be taken for granted. The Nazi understanding that "truth is what benefits the nation," or the Marxist view that "truth is what serves the proletariat," has implications both for political freedom and for the vitality of science, as we shall see later.

Finally, the extent of influence of the ethical attitudes of science on individual behavior may be questioned. The scientist as an individual is not necessarily more virtuous than other men; we have seen how varied are his motives, and must disavow the claim that he is invariably "humble, honest, dedicated only to truth." While working on a problem he is in fact completely absorbed in its technical details and gives little thought to anything else. The attitudes listed above operate less as personal motives than as presuppositions of the whole scientific enterprise and conditions of work embodied in its institutions and traditions.

"Disinterestedness," for example, turns out on further analysis to be more a feature of the scientist's occupational role than of his personal character. He is, in fact, likely to be intensely interested in his work, and to find in it both personal fulfillment and recognition. But "self-interest" does not fill the same overt function that it does in many jobs. The businessman is expected, according to *laissez-faire* ideology, to pursue his own profit, from which society will benefit indirectly. The scientist is not more altruistic than other men, but the rules of the game for achieving success are different.[6] The common welfare, represented by the development of science, is the focus of attention. The patterns approved by his colleagues do not sanction self-interest in the same way that they do traditionally in business, and the symbols of recognition are not primarily monetary. Many scientists do give up personal convenience and worldly pleasures, but less from any deliberate unselfishness than from interest in their work.

Attitudes which are present in the context of scientific work may be desirable elsewhere, but are not transferable in any easy way. Extravagant claims are sometimes made for the place of science in character formation. Even one course, we are told, teaches intellectual and moral virtues, and will instill in students "the ability to think straight," "absolute honesty of mind," "humility, tolerance, and goodwill." [7] But the studies that have been made suggest that attitudes learned in one field have limited influence on new situations in other fields; and outside their own area scientists can be as dogmatic as anyone else.

Thus on both the social and the individual levels the proposal of a simple transfer of the ethical attitudes of science appears to underestimate the complexity of ethical issues, to idealize the purity of the scientist's motives, and to provide no adequate dynamic for concern about the welfare of others. Scientific attitudes cannot be considered an adequate summary of religious ethics, in which justice and love surely transcend in both scope and power of motivation anything that science can provide. Nevertheless we shall see that all the attitudes implicit in research are indeed ideals which the Christian can affirm. He can try to practice and extend these values in all that he does, and yet be aware of their limitations as a total philosophy of life. He can be glad that the scientific enterprise does entail a moral structure, without claiming that these values are the research scientist's main contribution to mankind.

B. UNDERSTANDING GOD'S CREATION

A number of historians have stressed the contribution of the
Judaeo-Christian perspective to the rise of science. The biblical view of creation was one of the influences in the climate
of thought out of which scientific investigation arose. To be
sure, the Greek view of the rationality and orderliness of the
universe was also a major root of science. But Greek science,
though well developed in a few areas, never got very far in
others, in part because of lack of concern for detailed observation of the world. Its approach was primarily deductive in
trying to derive details from "first principles." In the biblical
perspective, God's rationality is reflected in nature; but he did
not have to form the precise sort of world he chose to create.
Man can understand the actual world only by investigating it
experimentally, not by thinking of a necessary rational structure which God would have had to follow. Nature is contin-
gent on the divine will and can be known only by observing
it humbly.[8] These were presuppositions from which science
could develop: the order, regularity, and intelligibility of nature, and the necessity of observation and experimentation.

Attitudes toward nature have always affected men's interest in investigating it. In Platonic thought, matter represented
a limitation, an imperfect embodiment of ideal forms; the material world was to be escaped in contemplation of pure ideas.
In many religions, nature has been either worshiped as divine,
divided among polytheistic forces, or seen as intrinsically evil.
In Hinduism, for example, the doctrine of Maya holds that
the natural world is essentially illusory; true reality is beyond
multiplicity and change. The biblical view, by contrast, considers creation fundamentally good; it takes a positive view
of the natural order and is concerned about events within history. There were, of course, many other factors that contributed to the rise of science, including trade, changing social

patterns, and Renaissance interests. But the fact cannot be ignored that it was in the Hebrew-Christian West alone among world civilizations that science was extensively developed.

It should be pointed out, however, that various strands within historical Christianity had widely differing influences on scientific research. There has been an ascetic theme of world-denial, attributable in part to Hellenistic thought in the early church, and expressed in some aspects of monasticism. By contrast, Puritan encouragement of "this-worldly" activity gave impetus to the growth of science as well as to the rise of capitalism, for men were urged to glorify God through good works. Most of the founding fathers of modern science were men of profound religious faith. On the other hand, biblical literalism and, to even a larger extent, the authority of Aristotelian cosmology retarded the acceptance of the work of Copernicus and Galileo. Nor should it by any means be implied that Christianity is the only world-view which can stimulate scientific research. Naturalistic humanism, for example, gives deliberate encouragement to this enterprise. But science would find little support in certain other philosophies, such as an extreme existentialism which deprecates man's reason and looks on the impersonal aspects of the universe as a meaningless stage for the drama of personal existence.

Throughout history there have been men who looked on their research as *studying God's handiwork* to his glory. Kepler spoke of his astronomical theories as "thinking God's thoughts after him." In the same spirit, William Pollard conceives the ultimate purpose of science as neither progress nor knowledge but the deepening of "the awed and appreciative wonder with which we respond to the work of God." He writes:

> Knowing that God's purpose in producing us within His creation is that this creation might have the means for

responding to Him, for praising and glorifying Him, we need only ask could it possibly be God's desire for us that we remain ignorant of all this deeper apprehension of His creation? . . . Science will piece together from it a far deeper and vastly wider apprehension of the wonder of God's creation than men two centuries ago could ever in their wildest fancies have guessed would be possible.[9]

This attitude of appreciation of the created order is in keeping with the biblical emphasis. The Hebrew people enjoyed nature in gratitude and wonder. The psalmist exults: "The heavens are telling the glory of God; and the firmament proclaims his handiwork" (Psalm 19:1). Man is given dominion over all things on the earth (Genesis 1:28) and science may be thought of as one form of such dominion.

Reverence for fact is required by this understanding of nature. The scientist must approach his material with humility, to learn and not to prescribe, with respect for the "givenness" of things and the integrity of the created order. He must be willing to be corrected in the light of the evidence regardless of his private convenience. Science is thus one form of self-transcendence, in which man is drawn out of himself in fidelity to the created order and finds his relationship to reality. Theory and observation are the two basic methodological components of science; whereas theory stresses the creative role of man's mind in constructing hypotheses, observation stresses the objective, "realistic" side of science, the given structures in terms of which hypotheses must be experimentally tested.

This appreciation of God's creation should be clearly distinguished from alternative views of the relation of religion to the work of the research scientist. Some Christians believe that God operates primarily by miraculous intervention in nature rather than in its regularities. This leads to the attempt to use God as an explanation for gaps in present knowledge. This "God of the gaps" is deprived of territory with each advance of science. In contrast, other scientists experience a sense of awe and mystery in relation to the known as much as to the unknown. Still others try to use the regularities of nature as proof of the existence of God, and argue that the evidence of purpose and design in the universe has been increased by modern knowledge. The Moody Bible Institute produces scientific films whose major theme is the evidence of design, a topic stressed also by the American Scientific Affiliation, most of whose members are conservative Christians with science Ph.D.'s. Men of more liberal theological viewpoints have also spoken of new discoveries as revealing God. C. A. Coulson, the Oxford mathematician, says that science is "helping to put a face on God"; it is "a definite religious activity, a revelation of God," and "one aspect of God's presence." [10]

These are significant affirmations, provided it is remembered that in the biblical perspective God is only partially revealed in the created order. Nature is an inadequate medium for the full disclosure of his purposes, which occurs in historical events and the lives of persons. The question "What does God have to do with *me?*" comes before the question "What does God have to do with *nature?*" "I-Thou" relationships are a more profound revelation of the divine than "I-It" relationships could be. Even when a man says that science led him to God, it was probably less a reasoned conclusion from the abstract symbols of technical knowledge than a total response to an experience of beauty, order, and reverence. It is in terms of such personal involvement, of which their work provided the context, that men in the laboratory have felt themselves to be in the presence of God.

The attempt to derive God from science leads at most to an impersonal Cosmic Force or a Great Designer. Sometimes God is equated with cosmic structure. Other thinkers (e.g., Schrödinger) [11] arrive at a pantheistic conception of God. Einstein goes further:

> A conviction, akin to religious feeling, of the rationality or intelligibility of the world, lies behind all scientific work of a high order. This firm belief in a superior mind that reveals itself in the world of experience represents my conception of God.[12]

The Hebrew-Christian conception of a personal God goes even beyond this. What we have been suggesting is that the individual who has come to know God in personal experience and in historic revelation can *then* view science as understanding God's creation, in which he has partially revealed himself.

A man's view of creation will, however, have an indirect rather than a direct influence on technical aspects of his work in the laboratory. Religious faith has nothing to say about the melting point of copper or the atomic weight of carbon. While working on a problem in biology one is completely absorbed in the immediate situation, and for the moment oblivious to its wider implications. The legitimate autonomy of science may be upheld from a biblical viewpoint, since the created order has its own relative independence. Respect for the given structure of reality means humility before the evidence. Moreover, freedom of inquiry, far from being limited by religious commitment, should be required by it. Radical honesty and dedication to truth are religious imperatives. We are free to follow the evidence wherever it leads. When the church has tried to dictate specific conclusions to scientists, it has misunderstood the nature of religious faith—and has often turned

Stephens College
Columbia, Missouri

out to be factually mistaken. The intellectual criteria of science are largely intrinsic to the discipline itself. Again, value-judgments are less directly involved in the details of work in the natural sciences than in many other fields; in the social sciences, for example, a scholar's work is more strongly affected by his views of the nature of man, his values and goals, and his perspective on society.

Although a man can carry out detailed investigations without asking philosophical and theological questions, religious faith is indirectly relevant to research. The prevailing world-view of a society does in the long run influence the presuppositions and values of scientific endeavor, as has been noted in the examples of dedication to truth and attitudes toward nature. In a day when practical results are extolled, and education becomes technical training, a Christian perspective may help undergird a profounder dedication to the pursuit of understanding in itself. Moreover, ethical decisions do arise even in connection with research. Selection of problems to investigate, and of questions that are considered valuable to ask, are indirectly influenced by the outlook of both the individual and the culture. Sometimes the probable consequences of a discovery can be foreseen sufficiently to involve the scientist in some degree of responsibility for the results of his work. A man's motivation and his view of the meaning and significance of his work are determined by his philosophy of life. Here Christianity is concerned less about the particular details of individual facts than about their relation to man's life and his goals.

C. The Use and Misuse of Reason

The two central elements in scientific activity are *observation* and *reason*. The former is more characteristic of the experimental side of research, the latter of its theoretical side. The biblical understanding of creation supports the empirical, observational aspect of science, but the Christian evaluation of the rational component seems more ambiguous. Whereas the Greeks exalted reason and considered the contemplation of truth the highest goal of man, biblical thought tended to value righteousness above truth or beauty. The truth in which it was interested was primarily the personal knowledge of God, persons, values and meanings, rather than the objective knowledge of the scientist. The Fourth Gospel asserts, "You will know the truth, and the truth will make you free" (John 8:32); but it goes on to refer to "doing the truth" and "the truth that is in Christ," stressing active participation rather than abstract contemplation or intellectual assent alone. Medieval scholasticism combined Greek and Hebrew emphases. Rationality, Aquinas maintained, is the distinctive characteristic of man, but is to be used to God's glory. Historians find the rise of science indebted to the legacy of the Middle Ages for belief in the intelligibility of the universe and faith in man's ability to understand.

Today Roman Catholic philosophy and Protestant Modernism affirm rationality as a high value in human life. Thus E. F. Caldin,[13] a British chemist with a Thomistic viewpoint, describes science as one version of the rational life, which is an essential part of the "good life." He upholds equally the role of reason in other areas, such as metaphysics and ethics, and suggests that use of intelligence in science develops self-discipline and understanding of rational procedures in general. Catholicism emphasizes reason in all fields, including philosophy of religion, while depending on revelation for the central truths of theology. Protestant Modernism, on the other hand, extols the power of reason throughout both science and theology.

Christian Existentialism and Fundamentalism, at the opposite extreme, tend to minimize the role of reason. Existentialists in general have little use for the detached impersonal analysis of objective inquiry, and reduce nature to the stage of man's personal life. Both Sartre and Kierkegaard disparage science. Fundamentalists have in the past sometimes considered both education and science to be works of the devil; this attitude, largely engendered by the controversy over evolution, is less common today. Milder forms of anti-intellectualism appear in defensiveness toward science among some Christians, and encouragement of piety in place of scholarship by some church colleges.

The main stream of Protestantism lies between the two extremes above. Here reason has an important but not an exclusive role within theology; historic revelation and personal experience must be interpreted, analyzed, and communicated by human reason. Attitudes toward rationality in theology and in science are not necessarily identical, and some authors make a sharp distinction by limiting the range of applicability of reason. More commonly the evaluation of reason in one area is reflected in a similar evaluation of its role in other areas. Respect for the scholar is characteristic of Judaism and Christianity. From the founding of the university in the Middle Ages to the establishment of colleges throughout America, the church has been a major sponsor of education.

God has given men minds to be used. "Whatever is true . . . whatever is just . . . think about these things" (Philippians 4:8). "Love the Lord your God with all your heart, and with all your soul, *and with all your mind*" (Mark 12:30). Jesus was obviously not referring specifically to science; but he was indicating that all aspects of man's life can express love of God. Serving God with the heart is important, as pietism reminds us; but serving God with the mind is the particular function of the intellectual life. Disciplined thought, responsible scholarship, and respect for truth are aspects of reverence for God, "the author of all truth."

The scientist's devotion to truth is an ultimate concern which he rightly feels as a sacred obligation. We can be thankful for this dedication even on the part of agnostic colleagues who do not see it as a form of worshiping God with the mind. Perhaps we can say of them what Paul said in the university town of Athens: "For as I passed along, and observed the objects of your worship, I found also an altar with this inscription, 'To an unknown god.' What therefore you worship as unknown, this I proclaim to you. The God who made the world and everything in it, being Lord of heaven and earth, does not live in shrines made by man. . . . Yet he is not far from each one of us, for 'In him we live and move and have our being' " (Acts 17:23–28).

The Christian can join forces with the scientist in looking on research as a form of rationality and fidelity to reality. Among philosophers of science the "idealists" emphasize the role of man's mind and the structure of ideas, while the "realists" emphasize the objective structure of the physical world. But only a few interpreters (e.g., the extreme "conventionalists") see scientific theories as arbitrary inventions of man's fancy. Even the person who wants to avoid the word truth and to speak only of "more adequate description and prediction" is acknowledging obligation to demands not of his own making. This represents a self-transcendence, and a loyalty to values, which contrast with contemporary moods of skepticism, cynicism, and meaninglessness.

Finally, Christianity has not only an affirmative word concerning rationality; it has also a word of caution about the temptations to which human reason is subject, and the ways in which man can misuse any of his powers:

1. *Intellectual pride.* The exhilarating experience of the mind's power can lead to an intellectual arrogance in which one sets oneself over against God and man. The optimism of

the eighteenth-century Enlightenment and its belief in inevitable progress can be traced in part to an exaggerated faith in man's intellect. More recent centuries have undermined this overconfidence. Freud showed how man's reason could be the servant of his unconscious desires—the very word "rationalize" reflects this ambivalence of rationality. Marx pointed to the role of cultural and class ideologies in many of our ideas. Man's inability to solve the problem of war has been a reminder of the strength of social irrationality. In the Christian tradition it has always been held that the central problems of man lie in his will and orientation, not in his intellect alone. Humility is high on the list of virtues, and nowhere is it more necessary than in the life of the mind.

2. *Intellectual narrowness.* There is a tendency for the specialist in any field to reduce all reality to the dimensions of his own field, and to elevate a partial view of reality into a total philosophy of life. The scientist needs to avoid too narrow a view of truth. Reason is often equated with technical analysis, and its role in other areas repudiated. In subsequent chapters we will look at the expressions of these dangers in particular situations: the limitations of scientific methodology as the teacher confronts them; the idolatry of science in contemporary society; and the temptation to identify science with the whole of reality in the scientist's own perspective.

3. *Intellectual irresponsibility.* Research is a fascinating pursuit and can easily lead to an ivory-tower existence, unconcerned with the relation of knowledge to the rest of the world. Involvement can be escaped by viewing problem-solving as an ultimate goal, as intriguing as a game of chess. The legitimate role of objectivity does not require neutrality on all issues. Even a university, whose primary service is to the truth, must not in the process neglect other values. The German universities expressed less opposition to the growth of Nazism in the 1930's than did the churches and labor unions;

their failure at this point has been attributed in large part to their neutral pursuit of truth without concern for the life of the nation.[14] By contrast, an example of intellectual responsibility occurred a few years ago when the University of Chicago was building a new cancer research hospital. It was believed that more patients would consent to undergo treatment if the wards were segregated racially. Some of the scientists said: "The only academic goal is the search for truth; we should have segregated wards if this will facilitate research." But the majority voted, in effect: "No, the university is committed to other values beside the pursuit of truth, and in this case the principle of racial equality is at stake." For a university as for an individual, the search for knowledge must never become an exclusive goal.

What can we conclude, then, concerning the Christian motivation for scientific research? Clearly one justification is that it leads to useful applications. It has often been pointed out that the United States has in the past been stronger in applied than in fundamental science, for which it has often been dependent on Europe. Radar, television, atomic energy, and antibiotics are a few of the many instances in which the U.S. has benefited from basic research done elsewhere. Moreover, pure science often issues in totally unexpected applications. Roentgen did not have in mind the healing of broken bones when he was investigating the properties of X-rays. A few years ago the New England fishing fleets were in despair because the fish were nowhere to be found; a biologist, who had been making a laboratory study of the temperature of fishes' stomachs, combined his data with some ocean temperature data and correctly suggested where the missing creatures might be found. Again, astronomy appears to be a "useless" subject, but has yielded a number of practical results, from the discovery of helium to the theories of the properties of gas plasma currently important in hydrogen fusion projects.

Yet most astronomers are not primarily interested in practical uses. Their motives include sheer enjoyment of and interest in astronomical problems, as well as curiosity and the desire to know. Even if no applications resulted, astronomy is an important enterprise for its contribution to our understanding of the universe in which we live. In an age dominated by Bacon's dictum that "knowledge is power," science is usually judged only in utilitarian terms. In this chapter we have tried to show that scientific research is a valid expression of the vocation to seek truth. It has been suggested that the Christian can affirm the ethical attitudes implicit in science; he can view his work as appreciation of God's handiwork; and he can prize rationality and the pursuit of knowledge. It is frequently said that the scientist should be interested in *"science for science' sake."* Taken literally, "for science' sake" appears to be meaningless, unless a cyclotron enjoys accelerating electrons or a law of physics is happy to be discovered. Taken as a caution against too great an emphasis on practical results, and a call to the values inherent in the search for truth, "science for science' sake" reflects an emphasis in which the Christian can join. But he might then prefer to say: *science for the sake of God and man,* for it is only in relation to God and man that these values are significant.

Chapter 4

THE SCIENCE TEACHER AND
THE STUDENT

THE TEACHER'S PRIMARY CHRISTIAN DUTY IS TO TEACH WITH competence, clarity, and imagination, awakening interest and encouraging understanding in his students. In high school, college, or university the science teacher is helping to prepare the scientists of the next generation. The inspiration and insights which he provides will be a major contribution to the future usefulness of his students.

While religious perspectives have nothing to do with the technical content of a lecture, they are relevant to a number of aspects of the academic situation.[1] Where appropriate to the objectives of the course and closely connected with the subject matter, some of the questions which we have raised about the effects of an invention on society or the ethical dilemmas faced by the scientist can legitimately be mentioned in the classroom. Religious commitment may also influence the teacher's attitudes concerning the methods of science, the philosophical and theological implications of certain topics, and the character of his relationships to students and faculty.

A. TEACHING THE METHODS OF SCIENCE

The modern world has been transformed by technology. Just as great has been the impact of science *as a way of thinking*. Though instruction concerning principles is the science teacher's primary function, he is also cast as interpreter of the scientific enterprise. He conveys indirectly, whether he intends to or not, his understanding of the process of scientific investigation. Some consideration of the methods, history, and philosophy of any field should be included, not as an addition to teaching the subject, but as integral to it. To the student who takes only one course in the natural sciences, an understanding of the ways in which science proceeds, and its significance for our culture, may be as valuable in later life as technical information acquired. The science major benefits also from conscious evaluation of methodology, even though he is continually exposed to the work of scientists. His ability to place his field of specialization within the context of a larger philosophy of life depends on a clear understanding of the nature of scientific endeavor and its relation to other human activities. These are questions about which the Christian should be particularly concerned.

The extent to which problems of method are mentioned will necessarily depend upon the objectives of the course. In a senior class in atomic theory they may enter seldom, though even in this field relativity and quantum mechanics did involve precisely such examination of basic assumptions. Too often only the final results of a discovery are taught, and no appreciation is gained of the process by which they were reached, or of the failures and blind alleys and first approximations involved in the investigation. At the other extreme, in a general-education biology course one might give rather frequent attention to what Conant calls "the strategy and tactics of science." [2] Some texts have gone so far in this direction that they have become books "about science," or present a smattering of so many fields that they end as superficial surveys. The "block-and-bridge" approach selects a few topics for intensive and rigorous study (preferably in one or at most two sciences) and sketches rapidly the connecting bridges between these blocks. Once the goal of encyclopedic coverage has been abandoned and there is no pressure to try to "get through all the material," some attention can be given to the strategy of science.

A number of physics texts, for example, give explicit attention to the methods of science and their limitations. A recent general physics book [3] includes chapters entitled "Understanding Science," "The Implications of Modern Physics," and "Science and Society" (the last, incidentally, devoting five pages to a section on "Science and Religion"). Another text discusses the limitations of science, concluding:

> The artist, the poet, the theologian, the philosopher, and the scientist—all have attempted parts of this description, and the work of each makes some contribution to the whole. . . . We shall see that the scientist limits himself professionally to certain aspects of the problem, and therefore cannot pretend that his description is complete. . . . The natural scientist confines himself in his description of the world to the objective data which he can obtain by the observation of nature.[4]

When such issues are treated only in the opening and closing sections of a course, students tend to look on them as addenda "tacked on" to the main body of subject matter. A more effective presentation considers methodological questions integrally with the more technical material, as is done in G. Holton's excellent volume.[5] Again, occasional use of the "case method" [6] allows the process of discovery to be seen in its total historical context, including social and intellectual forces. H. K. Schilling [7] suggests that the student should gain some picture of science as: a body of knowledge; a way of knowing; an area of experience; a foundation of technology; an intellectual and moral influence; and a social enterprise. For many teachers who were themselves narrowly trained, such approaches require considerable study on their own part in the history and philosophy of science, but the improvement in teaching is more than adequate reward.

Turning to specific methodological problems which might be raised in class, it should be noted that the activities of scientists have been far from uniform. There is no "scientific method" with five easy steps, as some interpreters imply; there are no do-it-yourself instructions for making discoveries! But there are some common characteristics of the process of investigation, such as:

1. *The interaction of hypothesis and experiment.* Observations lead to possible hypotheses and conceptual schemes; from these hypotheses, relationships which can be tested experimentally are deduced; the results may in turn suggest modifications or refinements in the theory. The teacher can bring out the role of inductive and deductive reasoning, the construction of conceptual schemes and models, idealization and simplifying assumptions, quantitative measurement and the controlled experiment. Of particular interest are the various criteria for evaluating alternative theories,[8] e.g., simplicity, consistency, and experimentally testable implications. Almost any area of discovery illustrates this process of interaction between hypothesis and experiment; among examples useful in elementary courses are the kinetic-molecular theory of gases, the geocentric-heliocentric debate in astronomy, the work of Galileo and Newton on motion, and Mendel's work on heredity.

2. *The creative character of scientific concepts.* Science is not just a matter of precise observation and the accumulation of facts. The concepts of valence and entropy are not given to us ready-made by nature, but are abstract interpretive constructions created in order to co-ordinate data, enabling us to trace coherent patterns. Schilling points out that in a sense the atom was "invented" as well as "discovered." A teacher can explain that the atom is not literally a group of electrons whirling like ping-pong balls around a nucleus, and that representation in wave equations is a symbolic mental construct used to organize and predict patterns of experimental relationship. Imagination and ingenuity have always been required, and advances have usually been the result of new ways of looking at old phenomena. Galileo's achievements were due not only to precision of observation but to the formulation of completely new concepts, such as that of acceleration. Men watched apples fall for centuries before Newton had the flash of insight from which he developed the law of universal gravitation.

3. *The social nature of science.* Science is a communal enterprise; there is no one-man science, for each person is dependent on predecessors and contemporaries. Most developments are a composite product, the cumulative result of many small discoveries or improvements. Scientists constitute a distinctive community with its own loyalties, standards, and institutions. The role of the Royal Society in early science, or of specialized journals today, can be pointed out. Science is also a part of the social order, influenced by practical needs, economic forces, and intellectual assumptions. The growth of astronomy was influenced by astrology and navigation; work on the properties of gases was stimulated by the need for better pumps; and more recently electronics and atomic physics have been developed in large measure for military purposes.

Many fundamental discoveries required instruments or equipment made possible only by technological or industrial activities.

The science teacher needs to have some insight into the limitations as well as the strengths of his field. These are limitations imposed by the nature of the scientific enterprise itself, not by some outside authority. Science is not infallible. Contrary to the popular impression, certainty is never achieved, and no formulation is final and irrevocable. A theory is never proven true; at best it is more useful, fruitful, comprehensive, and simple than alternative theories currently available. The chemist Arrhenius received the Nobel prize for his electrolytic theory of dissociation; the same prize was given later to Debye for showing the inadequacy of Arrhenius' scheme. Which of our present ideas will be modified by our children? Modern physics texts have been presenting the concept of parity or symmetry as one of the fundamental principles of nuclear structure. Those present at the 1956 physics meetings in New York will long remember the session in which two Chinese physicists reported results showing the untenability of this long-accepted principle.

Again, the methods of any science are necessarily selective. Every discipline develops its own symbolic language in terms of which it replaces the total complex situation by a model that represents those variables in which it is interested. In physics problems, an elephant on a river bank becomes a mass with a coefficient of friction, and a Beethoven symphony becomes a set of molecular vibrations. The scientist limits himself to sense-data, and prefers variables which can be measured and treated by the developed formalisms of mathematics. One of the foremost historians of science, Sir William Dampier, writes:

Physical science represents one analytical aspect of reality. . . . But the clear insight into its meaning which is given by modern scientific philosophy shows that by its inherent nature and definitions it is but an abstraction and that, with all its great and ever-growing power, it can never represent the whole of existence.[9]

If a scientific field can be more abstractive, its results will be more exact but further from ordinary life, and less adequately able to convey the immediacy, concreteness, and variety of human experience at all its levels. Furthermore, science is interested in repeatable events, reducible to general laws; it has no interest in that which is individual or unique, except as an instance of general laws. (By contrast, the historian must try to understand a unique pattern of events, which does not repeat itself; a novel, drama, or work of art cannot be reduced to general laws.) Students are quick to sense whether or not the teacher in any field recognizes the importance of other academic disciplines and other approaches to truth. Consideration of both the methods and the limitations of science is a significant classroom objective.

B. RELIGIOUS IMPLICATIONS IN SCIENCE COURSES

Scientific theories and principles seldom raise religious problems, and the teacher's world-view has little direct relevance for most of his lectures. Religion should never be extraneously brought into a discussion of technical issues. There are, however, occasional topics which have theological implications. The teacher's approach to such problems might start from three assumptions: (a) the teacher should be concerned with how science fits into the larger framework of life, and the student should raise questions about the meaning of what he studies and its relation to other fields; (*b*) controversial questions can be treated, not in a spirit of indoctrination, but with an emphasis on asking questions and helping students think through assumptions and implications; an effort should be made to present viewpoints other than one's own as fairly as possible, respecting the integrity of the student by avoiding undue imposition of the lecturer's beliefs; (*c*) presuppositions inevitably enter the classroom presentation of many subjects, so that a viewpoint frankly and explicitly recognized may be less dangerous than one which is hidden and assumed not to exist.

If these assumptions are valid, a Christian teacher may make clear to his class the way in which he himself is led by his religious commitment to a particular attitude on a problem that arises, provided he does so humbly, recognizing the fallibility of human interpretations and the ease with which we rationalize in favor of our own partial perspectives. He should indicate the major alternative viewpoints that are live options in our pluralistic culture; this may require an effort to inform himself concerning the current thought of scientists, theologians, and philosophers on the point at issue. He must also try to distinguish between evidence and interpretation, though recognizing that there is no sharp line between them. With this general approach in mind, let us look at an example from physics and then one from biology.

No two men are more significant in the history of physics, or assume more prominent positions in introductory courses, than Galileo and Newton. Not only their specific results in analyzing motion and force but also their methods of investigation make them the founders of physics as we know it today. Attention in class might well be called to some of the revolutionary methodological aspects of their work: the new combination of experiment and theory, the role of mathematical analysis, concentration on descriptive explanation (how a process occurs, not why), the prominence of the categories of space and time, invention of concepts not directly observable (e.g., acceleration), and the problem of freedom in science. But these men are important historically in a third way: not only their results and their methods but the philosophical interpretations of their ideas had a major impact on Western thought. Mention of some of these influences might appropriately be included in a physics course:

1. *Reality as matter in motion.* Galileo divided all attributes into two groups: "primary qualities" of mass and extension, which he believed to be properties of objects themselves, and all other "secondary qualities" such as color and hotness, which he believed to be merely subjective sensations in the observer's mind. He was attributing to external reality only those properties with which he as a physicist had been able to deal. E. A. Burtt calls this "constructing a metaphysics out of a method." "It was easier to get ahead in the reduction of nature to a system of mathematical equations by supposing that nothing existed outside the human mind not so reducible." [10] All causality was said to lie in the forces between atoms which alone constituted the real world. To explain anything meant to reduce it to its elementary parts. The influence of these assumptions was far-reaching; they were developed into the complete dualism of Descartes, the materialism of Hobbes, and the naturalism of the Age of Reason.

2. *The Newtonian synthesis and the Deistic conception of God.* The harmonious perfection of universal law, governing all motion from the smallest particle to the farthest planet, captured men's imagination. Newton and his colleagues saw this as evidence of order and design, bespeaking the beneficence of a purposeful Creator. Here was the basis of Deism in which God was pictured as the great designer, the cosmic

engineer, extolled in the familiar hymn of Newton's contemporary, Addison:

> The spacious firmament on high,
> With all the blue ethereal sky,
> And spangled heavens, a shining frame,
> Their great Original proclaim.
> Th'unwearied sun, from day to day
> Does his Creator's power display,
> And publishes to every land
> The work of an almighty hand.

3. *The development of determinism.* In the hands of later interpreters, particularly the writers of the French Enlightenment, the Newtonian world-machine was seen as deterministic and self-sufficient, the scene of purposeless and blind forces. The categories of physics, which had proved so powerful, were believed to be adequate to describe every aspect of man. Laplace claimed that if he knew the position and velocity of every particle in the universe, he could in principle predict all their future positions and hence all future events, governed by inexorable causal laws. The mechanical conception of nature continued to dominate science through the nineteenth century. Lord Kelvin stated that we do not really understand something until we can make a model of it. Illustrative of mechanistic thinking 75 years ago are the fantastic models of ether molecules devised to account for the properties of light transmission.

Reference to some of these outcomes of the Newtonian scheme is desirable not only because of their historical influence, but because the reaction of students to classical physics is likely to be similar to that of the generation following Newton. The teacher may wish to mention, either at this point or preferably later in the course, some of the modifications which twentieth-century physics has necessitated. Concerning *matter-in-motion,* it can be noted that mass, length, and velocity are in relativity no longer unchanging properties of objects in themselves. In quantum mechanics we have had to abandon continuous paths and perhaps the very concept of "position" as a property of a "particle." Moreover, analysis of systems into their smallest parts is no longer the main goal of explanation. The atom must be considered as a whole (in the wave-function of a 2-electron atom, even the separate identity of the electrons is lost). At higher levels, behavior must be analyzed as a total pattern rather than as an aggregate of parts.

Concerning *determinism,* Laplace's claim of universal predictability has been undermined by the Heisenberg Uncertainty Principle. Probability-distributions replace exact values of variables. The time at which an individual radioactive atom will disintegrate cannot be calculated. Most physicists believe that these indeterminacies reflect fundamental aspects of atomic structure rather than temporary deficiencies in man's knowledge. This gives no simple solution to the problem of human freedom, however, as has been indicated elsewhere.[11] Concerning *mechanical models,* it can be noted that in many areas of physics we now use abstract mathematical representations which cannot be visualized at all. Moreover, a scientific theory is seldom looked on today as an exact reproduction or replica of nature "as it is in itself." The neat distinction between observer and observed breaks down. We deal with relationships, not objects in themselves; note the role of the observer's frame of reference in relativity, or his disturbance of the system in atomic experiments. Thus mechanistic and deterministic philosophies can find less support from modern than from classical physics.

The most obvious example of religious implications in biology is the topic of evolution.[12] In the debate over the relation of Genesis to the Darwinian theory of natural selection there have always been several views of the Bible. On the one hand are those who look on Scripture as completely divine, its authors having taken dictation from God. A clergyman holding this belief in verbal inspiration suggested that "God put misleading fossils in the rocks to test the faith of man." Some biologists try to preserve a modified form of scriptural inerrancy by quoting the verse "a day is as a thousand years," and then showing that after all Genesis agrees fairly well with evolution. The Roman Catholic position is that the human body may have evolved gradually, but the first human soul was created in a separate act of God. At the opposite extreme are those who look on the Bible as completely human, a record of man's history in which God had no part. Genesis is dismissed as a primitive fable from a pre-scientific age. A middle position sees the biblical record as neither completely divine nor completely human, but as involving both God and man; its authors conveyed profound insights into the nature of God, but expressed this religious message in poetic form and in terms of the understanding of the world then current.

In this view, which is the dominant one in Protestantism today, the message of Genesis is that man and the world are dependent on God, that the created order is purposeful and good, and that God is free and sovereign. The scientific details of the history of nature were not what the Bible was trying to convey, and these we must learn from science. The doctrine of creation is fundamentally a statement that all existence depends upon God, an affirmation which is compatible with various scientific theories of how the details of creation were and are being accomplished. In Genesis this religious message is cast in terms of the cosmology of the ancient world; today it must be coupled with whatever cosmological view is scientifically most tenable. One might say that evolution was a part of the process by which God created. What the biblical understanding of creation rules out is not any scientific account, but other interpretive statements, such as "God is nature" (pantheism), "the world is essentially unreal" (Hinduism), "matter is ultimate" (materialism), or "the world is evil" (Schopenhauer—and some forms of existentialism).

The fact that evolution has taken place is clear, as well as the broad outlines of its history, but there are some unresolved problems still under debate among biologists. Are favorable mutations abundant enough to provide, in the time available, the variations which natural selection would require (mutations from ionizing radiations appearing to be both too rare and too predominantly unfavorable)? How can one account for the elimination of unused organs that are in no way detrimental (e.g., the eyes of cave animals), or cases where an advantage would be gained only by the simultaneous occurrence of a large number of modifications, each of which is detrimental by itself (e.g., factors in the nesting pattern of the cuckoo bird)? Such instances, for which no convincing scientific explanations have been given, are cited by some Christian biologists as evidence of God's intervention in the process. This interpretation can be criticized on scientific grounds because it tends to discourage the search for further understanding. It can also be criticized theologically as a continuation of the "God of the gaps," attempting to invoke God as explanation for an area of ignorance. Historically this has been a rear-guard action which has surrendered further territory as new areas are explored. Newton's astronomical data were slightly in error, so that he believed God not only started the planetary machine but had to readjust it periodically; but more accurate data seemed to leave the Divine Engineer unemployed! C. A. Coulson puts the issue clearly: "When we come to the scientifically unknown, our correct policy is not to rejoice because we have found God; it is to become better scientists." [13]

Rather than looking for God's intervention at certain points, we can speak of God's activity through the process as a whole, in the purpose evidenced by its direction and in the appearance of organization out of chaos. Here the element of design and purpose is built into the materials and conditions, the chemical properties and biological laws necessary for higher forms of life. The amazing thing is that because of what L. J. Henderson called "the fitness of the environment," random events (which should, by definition, yield chaotic and random results) can contribute to a creative and directional development. Moreover, *mechanism* and *purpose* (teleology) are not mutually exclusive categories in looking at either the behavior of a man or the evolution of the universe; we need to ask about both the mechanics of a process and its purpose.

A related problem concerns the possibility of deriving ethics from evolution. C. H. Waddington,[14] the British biologist, argues that "science can provide a secure basis for ethics by discovering and exhibiting reality to be an evolutionary process tending in a certain direction, action in conformity to which is to be taken as right conduct." There are several difficulties in this idea which is common among biologists. Why should man follow the pattern of nature? Julian Huxley believes that man should co-operate because evolution evidences co-operation. But his grandfather, T. H. Huxley, believed man should co-operate for exactly the opposite reason: human ethics, he said, must be precisely *the denial of* the ethics of nature, which he saw as a ruthless struggle, "red in tooth and claw." A physicist suggests that ethics can be derived from the principle of entropy, since it is imperative for all men "to fight always as vigorously as possible to increase the degree of order in their environment so as *to combat the natural tendency* for order in the universe to be transformed into disorder." [15] Besides this fundamental question of whether we are to look to nature for what we should do or for what we should not do, there are no criteria in this approach for any ethical discrimination between cases of mutual aid and of cruelty, both of which occur in nature. Nor does this theory provide any clear answer to the question: Now that further evolution in man is partially subject to his conscious control, toward what goals should he influence future human development? The attempt to derive ethics from evolution raises a number of issues which could legitimately be mentioned in a biology course.

C. Relationships to Students and Faculty

In the science teacher's relationship to the student in the classroom the subject matter is always central. To be sure, the teacher is not just dispensing information. Education is an encounter between persons, but it is an encounter in relation to a subject. The personal factor is thus highly significant without being the direct focus of attention; though the whole person is the context, the life of the mind is the immediate concern. Education is not a dialogue, as in a counseling situation. Nor, on the other hand, is it a hierarchy in which the student is subordinate to the teacher handing down truth to him. Instead, both student and teacher are always subordinate to the demands of truth. Concern for the student as a person, which is required by both sound educational practice and religious faith, must thus in the classroom take forms related to the learning process itself. For instance, blocks to understanding are sometimes as much emotional as intellectual. A teacher's sensitivity to what is going on in the student's mind may require tolerance, patience, and imagination—or, at other times, enthusiasm or even an intellectual jolt to overcome apathy. Effective communication depends on the teacher's vision, not alone of his subject and its relevance, but of the learner's potentialities for appreciation and understanding. Concern for the individual also means respect for his integrity, and caution about "classroom imperialism"; it is all too easy to try to mold students in one's image and use them for one's own ends.

A science teacher is a person and not just a scientist. As a man he recognizes aesthetic and ethical values; he is an artist and a philosopher as well as an instructor in technical principles. As a Christian he should treat his subject no less rigorously for the fact that he looks on the created order with reverence and wonder, which will be communicated indirectly to his students. In advising students outside the classroom he must avoid imposing his ideas if he is to help the counselee think through his own situation. Often the counseling relationship extends beyond academic matters, and the teacher exercises a sort of "pastoral" function. His concern is not just for the technical ability of the student, but for all the levels of his life—the pressures of conformity, his uncertainties and confusions, his emerging image of himself and his role. The faculty adviser can help a student find opportunities, both in choice of courses and elsewhere, to think through his own philosophy of life. The total influence of a teacher is the sum of many actions, from a discussion over a cup of coffee, to assumption of campus and community responsibilities. The Jacob study [16] found student attitudes and values influenced by two factors: a few outstanding professors whose personality affected their lives; and the prevailing climate of opinion or ethos of the campus. A teacher determines the atmosphere of the classroom, but he also influences the goals and norms of the academic community.

The teacher is also a member of a larger faculty. Ideally a university or college is an integral enterprise, a community of common inquiry. More characteristic of most colleges, however, is specialization and fragmentation. A university president described his institution as "a collection of departments connected by plumbing." Scientists and non-scientists are frequently in intellectual isolation from each other. There are many barriers to communication, such as lack of common knowledge and interests, or differences in the logic of discourse and criteria of meaning in various fields. Some of the reluctance to enter into real dialogue stems from insecurity in relation to other faculty members. We are hesitant to expose our ignorance outside our field; we retreat to territory in which we remain experts and can speak our own jargon. Here the Christian faith offers insight concerning anxieties about status in the eyes of others; in the experience of a new relationship to God and man, a person can be freed from excessive self-defensiveness. The Christian sense of the oneness of truth and of mutual dependence can also make us more willing to learn from each other.

Specific interdisciplinary projects can assume many forms. Coming to know colleagues socially and in personal friendship often leads to interaction at the level of ideas, though this does not result automatically. Participation in common problems relating to the intellectual life of the campus can encourage fruitful exchange. Interdepartmental seminars, or courses representing bridges between disciplines, can aid the integration of specialized knowledge by faculty as well as students. Faculty research clubs on some campuses have facilitated encounter with the creative work of colleagues, and informal discussions have dealt with the methods of various fields and their assumptions. (What view of the nature of man is implicitly taught in our various departments? At what points do value-judgments enter each discipline?) In a faculty characterized by both pluralism of viewpoints and mutual tolerance and respect, such common explorations can be rewarding.

Every faculty member has a part in planning the curriculum. Most colleges require some work in science of all students. Should "general education" courses be provided, and should more than one field be included? Some of the advantages of a "block-and-bridge" course over an "elementary survey" have already been suggested. Other problems arise in planning requirements for science majors. How can a student include all the courses necessary for competence in his field, and yet avoid becoming a narrowly specialized technician? Most universities require science majors to take work in the humanities and social sciences; M.I.T., Cal. Tech., and other high-ranking technical schools have substantial requirements in these areas. Exposure to critical thought in regard to social and ethical issues is desirable because of the role such problems will assume in the scientist's later activities, and also because technical schools tend to be so closely associated with industry that a student can easily acquire an uncritical version of "the American business creed" without ever having really thought about it.

Science majors, along with other students, should confront the perennial questions about the nature of man, God, and the goals of life, and some of the diverse answers which have been given. An academic institution has a responsibility to help each student in the development of his philosophy of life. Our colleges, founded in the name of truth, have often become exponents of success; we turn out graduates without convictions, conformists whose actions are determined by what other people are doing. Nor can Western civilization be adequately understood without some knowledge of its Greek and Hebrew roots and the religious tradition which has played so large a part in its history and thought. Some orientation in time is a mark of an educated man.

The U.S. reacted to Sputnik with action to improve science teaching in schools and universities. This reaction was justified, but it runs the danger that other fields will be neglected. The goal should be the education of *every* student up to his capacities—not just the potential scientist. Some observers are apprehensive about the outcome if there is further increase in the trend for most of the best minds of our country to go into science. With the tremendous prestige of modern technology and with financial help coming from industry and government, there is pressure even on liberal arts colleges to become technical schools. Without lessening support for the natural sciences, the humanities and social sciences must also be strengthened. We have been suggesting that the teacher may derive from his religious faith both greater sensitivity to persons and active concern for the total educational process.

Chapter 5

SCIENCE AND THE SOCIAL ORDER

IN EARLIER CHAPTERS, THE SCIENTIST'S VOCATION TO SERVE human need and to seek truth was discussed; some of the opportunities of the science teacher have also been suggested. A further aspect of the vocation of every Christian is the call to work for a better society. Christian ethics is concerned not just about individuals but about the quality of corporate life. Often the institutional context of a discovery such as atomic energy determines its consequences for mankind. This chapter deals with the place of science in the social order, and the channels through which the scientist can responsibly contribute to the formation of public policy.

Many of the critical choices today are made by groups, and there are many points at which scientists participate in such decision-making processes. In industry they often enter into the councils of management. In government they serve as advisers to the armed forces, legislative committees, and overseas embassies. In the agencies of the United Nations, technical experts have been active in world-wide planning. Some act through professional societies, such organizations as Academies of Science, such groups as the Federation of Atomic Scientists, or local committees. For a few, participation in public life may be a full-time job as "scientist-statesmen" (e.g., Conant, Bush, Killian). Many others exert their influence as individuals through public channels of information and discussion. Those who do not want to curtail their research work can find opportunities as citizens, in church and civic groups, and in political parties.

In participating in policy decisions the scientist will be acting outside his field of specialized competence, and some cautions are in order. He can easily oversimplify the social problems which his restricted education has prevented him from studying. Having great faith in reason, he may assume that a logical proposal is all that is needed. A biologist states, for example, that "scientific evidence of the unity of the human race will overcome race prejudice." "We should replace violence with intelligence" is the helpful advice of a physicist. A study of the political philosophy of scientists [1] finds that they seldom recognize the diversity of interests present in group situations or the processes of negotiation by which compromises must often be reached. The dangers of naïveté outside his field of competence should not, however, discourage a person from trying to act responsibly on public issues. There will be situations in which his specialized knowledge will be particularly valuable, provided he makes an effort to inform himself about the human aspects of the question. A sampling of such issues is given in this chapter.

A. FREEDOM IN SCIENCE AND SOCIETY

For its greatest vitality the scientific enterprise requires freedom to choose and pursue problems, to publish and discuss results, and to criticize any theory. Research must be judged by the scientific community in terms of its own criteria, not by any external authority in terms of prescribed ideologies. Restrictions of its independence have usually been detrimental to its progress. This has occurred when ecclesiastical authority has attempted to prescribe its conclusions, as in Galileo's trial by the Inquisition. In Nazi Germany, scientific development was considerably weakened in a dozen years by political control of universities and laboratories and the promotion of "Aryan science."

Russian science has suffered in those areas which were subjected to political pressures, of which the most dramatic was Lysenkoism in biology. Since Stalin's death, however, science has been given top priority in financial allotment, in the educational system, and in salaries and public prestige; in addition, the climate of work has improved, and most of those exiled or disgraced have been rehabilitated. Young scientists have been observed to criticize theories of distinguished members of the academy. An American physicist reports: "We have clear evidence that the Soviet government now understands that genuine scientific progress requires scientific freedom." [2] Whether liberty within science will exert an influence toward political liberty is more questionable.

In America, the chief restriction of freedom in science has been excessive secrecy in security measures. Some areas of research are seriously handicapped because people do not know which problems have been investigated already and the results "classified." There have been harmful practices in loyalty investigations. We noted in the Oppenheimer case the failure to distinguish clearly between dissent, indiscretion, and disloyalty. Other scientists have been refused clearance without ever being allowed to know or reply to the charges. Analyzing hysteria and hyperpatriotism in American life, Edward Shils concludes that we have tended to see things in black and white:

> Since all that is not white is not obviously black, it must be "really" black in the sense that it hides its darkness under a disguise. . . . Anxiety about conspiracy

brings with it a distortion of the conception of individual liberty.... Conspiracy is conceived not necessarily as oriented toward the performance of specific
acts, but as the harboring of certain states of mind.[3]

Both loyalty review boards and Congressional investigating
committees serve legitimate purposes, but they have often
assumed the functions of court trials without the attendant
safeguards. The fundamental assumption of innocence until
proven guilty has been seriously compromised; many a man
has been cast under suspicion by being investigated, and
then the case has been dropped without any statement clear-
ing him.

In the academic world, freedom may be jeopardized in
many ways. There have been demands to dismiss faculty
members whose viewpoints were unpopular or to ban controversial visiting speakers, and pressures from industry for
the university to serve particular interests. In April, 1956, the
American Association of University Professors voted to
censure six institutions for violations of academic freedom,
most of them in loyalty procedures. Intellectual integrity may
also be more subtly endangered from within by the mold of
conformity or by avoidance of controversial issues. In industry, secrecy in research is often the result of commercial
competition. One of the purposes of the patent system is to
allow free exchange of information while protecting a company's investment in a new process, but it has only partially
fulfilled this function.

The limitation of scientific freedom by the planning and
co-ordination of science is more problematical. No one
directed Newton's work or told Mendel to discover laws of
heredity; creative work seems to elude regimentation, whether
in research or in great music and art. But there is a process

of automatic co-ordination which, as Polanyi has pointed out,[4] does not endanger freedom because it is the scientific tradition which governs individual efforts. A person obeys the moral authority of his peers because he shares their standards, values, and goals, and the dedication to truth that is implied in the operation of science. The arbiter is the voluntarily acknowledged judgment of scientific opinion. The self-government of science has its own institutional structures which embody its standards and enforce its discipline. The decisions of journal editors, committees reviewing applications for grants, and administrators making appointments, all serve as informal ways of planning. But these processes could not co-ordinate individual activities if there were not already a widespread coherence of voluntary loyalties.

A more formal type of planning, however, appears to be increasingly necessary. Team projects are common today and require careful organization. In most industries, company directives control group projects, though the most outstanding laboratories allow considerable individual initiative. The cost of equipment in some fields, such as high-energy physics, and the new role of the government in providing support demand the advance programing of research. Further, the extent to which a democratic society should guide and control the activities of science has been the subject of vigorous discussion, particularly in England. Scientists oriented toward socialism or Marxism (e.g., Bernal, Needham, Haldane) have complained that within capitalism the direction of science has been determined by corporation profits rather than the public welfare.[5] The solutions they offer stress political controls, which run the risk of imposing particular ideologies on the structure of science. Emphasis on the social utility of science also tends to lead to the neglect of pure science. Clearly they are right that the public has a crucial stake in the scientific enterprise, whose general direction at least should be a matter of national policy, for example in the allotment of federal funds. But the administration of such funds should perhaps be in the hands of scientists themselves and as free from political pressures as possible.

The Christian perspective can illuminate this tension between freedom and order. Believing in the worth of the individual and the basic equality of all men in the sight of God, we are led to seek the fulfillment of free persons in the context of community. But the understanding of liberty here is not primarily negative (freedom *from* restraint), but positive (freedom *for* self-determination and responsible choice). Again, a realistic estimate of man requires the establishment of democratic political mechanisms; man is good enough to govern himself, but evil enough that no individual or group can be trusted with absolute power. As Reinhold Niebuhr puts it, "Man's capacity for justice makes democracy possible, but his inclination to injustice makes democracy necessary."[6] Christian concern for justice and for human relationships takes one even further from "rugged individualism," toward provision of structures of order within which freedom can be creative. And if we believe that God seeks man's voluntary commitment, religious freedom is also essential.

Both as scientists and as Christians we have reasons to work for a social order providing the maximum freedom consistent with the operation of justice and equality. Restrictions of political liberty tend to be reflected in restrictions on science. Moreover, the premises of freedom within the scientific tradition imply wider freedoms; a culture which believes in the universality of truth and shares a common dedication to it will encourage freedom of discussion, rather than the settlement of arguments by force. Modern technology in turn adds urgency to concern for democratic processes. Tolstoy wrote prophetically: "If the arrangement of society is bad and a small number of people have power over the majority and oppress it, every victory over Nature will inevitably serve only to increase that power and that oppression." One aspect of the vocation to work for a better society, then, is the preservation and extension of freedom both in science and in political life, without neglecting the requirements of order and justice.

B. The Worship of Technology

What should be the role of science among the goals of the social order? Power over nature has always been one of the motives for seeking technical knowledge, linking it in function with the practice of magic in earlier days. In the public image the scientist is the white-coated high priest of the new order, the guardian of its secrets. His work is the infallible oracle, the guarantor of the advertisement: "Science says. . . ." While he himself may have various motives, he is sought by others primarily because of the economic, military, and political power which he mediates. William Pollard sees technology today as a Promethean quest for human self-sufficiency, omnipotence, and complete mastery over nature, a celebration of man's glory rather than God's. "No more terrible affront to the Creator could be made by man than this all-out determination to seize God's creation from Him and make himself sovereign within it." [7] Yet surely it is not power itself that must be condemned, but the ways in which men misuse it.

The sense of power which science brings is perhaps most tempting and most dangerous in the manipulation of people. The control of human behavior in the interests of efficiency presents frightening possibilities, conveyed vividly by Huxley's *Brave New World* or Orwell's *1984*. But this same tendency toward depersonalization and mechanization has been a widespread concomitant of modern technology. Our culture is increasingly the servant of external, technical interactions of control and manipulation (what Buber calls "I-It" relationships) to the neglect of personal response to people as subjects ("I-Thou" communication). Persons should be ends, and things means, not vice versa. We are called to love people and use objects, rather than loving objects and using people. The machine tends to set the pace for man, requiring him to adapt his schedule to its needs. Somehow the machine can take possession of man's life, and the relation of the craftsman to his work is lost. Mass advertising of mass-produced goods exerts a pressure toward uniformity and conformity.

Today there is a widespread belief that science will solve all problems, and that luxury and prosperity are the prime object of life. The mass media extol greater comfort and easier living; the assumption is that human needs are exclusively material. American activism is concerned to get things done, and "know-how" is more likely to be valued than "know-why." Efficiency becomes an end in itself, even if it is efficiency in achieving inadequate goals. In analyzing these effects of technology it is difficult, however, to distinguish between those which are inherent in scientific advance and those which are the result of a particular historical situation. The introduction of technology inevitably accelerates cultural change, which almost always leads to personal instability and social disorganization. On the other hand, the leisure that greater efficiency brings may or may not be desirable, depending on the values of a particular group. In some situations leisure may be used creatively, whereas in others it may lead only to new ways to kill time.

The reaction of the Christian to a technological civilization is likely to be both appreciative and critical. The biblical tradition does not minimize the value of material progress. It is not otherworldly or interested only in a future life, for it is deeply concerned about the conditions in which men live now. Calling a halt to scientific work would not remedy the basic problem of modern man, and backbreaking scarcity would be no more "spiritual" in its impact than an economy of abundance. But biblical religion does speak out when material progress becomes the source of meaning and purpose in life. It criticizes not science in itself but an unqualified devotion to goals identified with the products of science. Technology as a total way of life becomes idolatry, that is, ultimate allegiance to something less than God. Man is insecure and tries to build a pattern of life that will disguise his insecurity; attempting to escape the threat that life might be meaningless, he organizes his values around inadequate centers of meaning. When technology becomes such a center, he ends as a slave to his own material comforts. As Augustine saw, a person's life is determined by what he loves.

Exclusive preoccupation with technology can thus warp attitudes to nature, to God, and to man. Nature is looked on as an alien order to be exploited and plundered, with no sense that it is a kindred creation to be appreciated and enjoyed. In rebellion against God, new achievements offer new opportunities for the kind of intellectual pride and self-sufficiency which encourages us to exalt ourselves and try to get along without him. Any distortion of values also injures human relationships. In the biblical perspective, progress is to be measured in terms of the quality of man's life, his moral and spiritual stature, his corporate existence in community. "If I understand all mysteries and all knowledge . . . but have not love, I am nothing" (1 Corinthians 13:2). Shortly after the first Sputnik, a *New York Times* editorial affirmed:

The greatest adventure of all is not to go to the moon or to explore the rings of Saturn. It is rather to understand the heart and soul of man and to turn away from wrath and destruction toward creativeness and brotherly love.[8]

The goal of Christian ethics is the fulfillment of the lives of persons in community. Today this requires a reassertion of the distinctively human values, such as personal responsibility and individual creativity. The capacities of human nature which are not immediately "useful" must be cultivated; appreciation of beauty and dedication to truth and goodness must find expression. (Even art and philosophy have too often become essentially technical exercises, analysis predominating over synthesis, skill over purpose, form and language over content.) Those who affirm the primacy of person-to-person relationships and the necessity of understanding, compassion, and forgiveness will give attention to the life of the family, small groups, and the church. This leads, not to a repudiation of technological progress, but to the attempt to ensure that the technical aspects of man's life do not predominate over his personal and interpersonal existence.

Finally, the organized church can respond to modern civilization in several possible ways. H. Richard Niebuhr has traced five types of strategy which Christians through the centuries have adopted as they tried to relate Christ and culture.[9] At the risk of oversimplification, we could extend and paraphrase these classifications as they might apply to the interpretation of contemporary technology by the church:

1. *"Religion against Science."* This view condemns science as lust for power and comfort; technology is denounced as materialistic and dehumanizing. It is asserted that the church

should *withdraw from* an evil scientific culture and attempt to preserve her own patterns of uncompromising perfection in the simpler life of an earlier day. (This is the answer of the Amish and other separatist religious communities.)

2. *"Religion under Science."* This is the way of accommodation to prevailing attitudes. The church should *adapt to* a technological culture, selecting the best from all fields of human endeavor. We are asked to apply the methods of science to all areas including religion. This view tends to be as optimistic about man and his progress as the first view is pessimistic. (This position may be taken consciously by extreme liberalism, and unconsciously by those who have lost all distinctive religious beliefs and the ability to criticize the values of their culture.) In the first view, religion is supreme and tends to reject science; in the second, science is supreme and tends to absorb religion. Between these extremes are three attempts to preserve a balance:

3. *"Religion above Science."* Science is valuable but can deal with only limited areas of knowledge; the most important truths come from revelation, and theology is queen of the sciences. We should seek a new "Christendom," a modern version of the medieval synthesis. The church should have *control over* technology both in ideas and institutions. Here the balance of science and religion is preserved institutionally. (This is a thumbnail sketch of the main Roman Catholic emphasis.)

4. *"Religion separate from Science."* Religion has to do with individual salvation; the church should not become involved in the problems of technological civilization. Life in the world has to be governed by a different code of ethics from that applicable to personal life. The two areas are *watertight compartments* with respect to ideas, values, and institutions. Here the balance between science and religion is preserved by keeping them apart, so that each has its own

sphere of operation. (Luther and Barth at times reflect such a double standard, and many Christians in practice live by a separation of religion from daily life.)

5. *"Religion transforming Science."* Religious faith and a technological culture interact not primarily as institutions, but as aspects of the life of individuals. Scientists have complete freedom to investigate, but decisions about the purposes science should serve involve essentially religious questions concerning the meaning of life and the goals of men. The church can *reorient* society through the redirection of men's values, enabling them to be sensitive to the worth of persons, to respond with concern for their needs, and to establish corporate structures of justice. (Some of these themes can be found in Calvin and Wesley.)

This fifth approach is implied in the earlier suggestion that the scientist responds as a free person to a total situation which includes God, human needs, and technical data. In this view the church makes no absolute claims and assumes no temporal authority, for it too stands under God's judgment. It is, however, in dialogue with society, helping men wrestle with social problems. The dynamic interaction works both ways, for religion must also re-evaluate itself in the light of new knowledge. The Christian must admit that he is himself a product of a technologically oriented culture, whose values he has to some extent absorbed. Yet he is not totally immersed in it, for the biblical tradition gives him an independent standing-ground from which he can judge his society. He can work for scientific progress without becoming its slave, and he can discriminate among the purposes technology may serve.

Each of these five approaches emphasizes a valid element in the Christian tradition, and there may be historical circumstances in which each is particularly appropriate. The strategy of *withdrawal* (#1 above) maintains in a dramatic form the prophetic witness against social evils; under a totalitarian government it may be the only way in which the church can exist at all. In contemporary America, however, it preserves the church's internal integrity at the expense of responsibility for the wider community. *Accommodation* (#2) can easily lose the distinctive message of the gospel, while the *institutional* approach (#3) tends to impose a particular ideological synthesis and to absolutize one ecclesiastical pattern. *Compartmentalization* (#4) has no effective impact on corporate life. Only the attempt to transform society from within (#5) can redirect a technological civilization to the service of God and man, preserving a legitimate place for scientific progress without making it the ultimate source of meaning in life. A culture having profound respect for human personality will pursue technology, not as an end in itself but as a means of serving the genuine needs of men.

C. SCIENCE AND NATIONAL POLICY

We turn now to some current issues of science in national policy in which there may be significant opportunities to work for a better society. The examples represent *one* person's response at a particular time (1960), and are not meant to prescribe "*the* Christian answer" for all time. Characteristic of such issues is the way in which technical and moral questions are intertwined. The recent fall-out controversy provides a case study of this interaction of scientific data with political and ethical judgment. The public has been confused by the fact that eminent experts have contradicted each other concerning biological dangers from nuclear tests. Pauling has said that the situation is "alarming," and 9,000 scientists including 36 Nobel-prize winners signed a petition in 1958 calling for a halt to weapons testing. On the other hand, Teller

stated that there is "negligible danger," and the Atomic
Energy Commission has issued reassuring statements.[10]
There are several reasons for the disagreement:

1. *Differences in scientific data.* Where adequate facts are
not available, or where there is a range of plausible estimates
(e.g., the effect of low-level radioactivity on bone cancer),
one side makes the more optimistic assumptions, the other the
more pessimistic. One side uses average values; the other allows
for wide variations from averages. Moreover, the same facts
can be presented in various ways. The alarmists speak of
10,000 new leukemia cases annually if testing continues at
the present rate; those who would reassure us say this would
be a rise of only one-half of 1 per cent, which is "a negligible
percentage." At hearings in May, 1959, the AEC estimated
that Strontium-90 already released will produce only 300
cases of leukemia and bone cancer annually in the U.S. But
this is equivalent to saying that from past tests alone 140,000
such victims will die throughout the world in a generation
(the half-life of Sr-90), quite apart from genetic damage or
effects of C-14 and I-131.

2. *Differences in comparisons of danger.* Teller finds the
hazards small relative to the 40,000 annual deaths in auto
accidents. Pauling replies that this is "a highly immoral com-
parison," since the latter is a voluntarily assumed risk. Again,
we are told that radiation from Sr-90 has been less than
common exposures from medical X-rays. But this statement
is less reassuring since a careful British study found that if
a mother was X-rayed during pregnancy, the child is about
twice as likely to die of a malignant disease before its 10th
birthday.[11] Harrison Brown summarizes the problem:

> A person who subscribes to the AEC philosophy might
> phrase the effect of continuing testing upon the incidence
> of leukemia as follows: "This effect is so small that it

cannot be detected with certainty in death statistics. Clearly the risk is far less than most other risks which we face as payment for our pleasure, our comfort, or our material progress." Many of us, however, might prefer to phrase the consequences in other terms: "Continued testing at the present rate may well result in the death each year from leukemia of nearly 10,000 persons who might not otherwise have died." [12]

If there is a human cost for *any* increase in radiation, the decision is a moral and social as well as a technical one. There is no scientific standard for measuring the value of a human life.

3. *Differences in political context.* This is the basic reason for the dispute. Teller feels strongly that no agreements with Russia are possible. He considers the H-bomb, of which he has been called "the father," to be the only deterrent to nuclear war; compared to all-out war, any loss of life from testing is insignificant. The AEC has the development of H-bombs as its main assignment, so it is not surprising that it has minimized fall-out dangers and opposed test ban negotiations. Pauling, on the other hand, believes that a workable plan to limit testing could be the opening wedge to lessen tensions and develop further international controls. Taking the present dangers seriously might produce the first steps in halting the nuclear race, which he sees as leading only to disaster.

While there has been controversy about testing, there is no dispute as to the magnitude of the catastrophe of actual nuclear warfare. One bomb now carries more destructive energy than all the explosives used in all wars throughout history. It is estimated that present nuclear stockpiles contain the equivalent of 10 tons of TNT for every human being

on the globe. Two hundred and fifty bombs would kill half
the U.S. population,[13] and several hundred million more
might die from delayed effects somewhere in the world; industrial civilization as we know it, and possibly man's genetic
inheritance as a species, would disappear. Even the so-called
"clean" H-bombs, in addition to the immediate casualties they
would create, produce appreciable quantities of radioactivity.
Punch commented:

> To call the H-bomb clean
> makes sound and sense divergent
> unless it's meant to mean
> The Ultimate Detergent.[14]

No one would "win" a future war. The only alternatives
today are co-existence or co-nonexistence.

The policy of deterrence and "brinkmanship" cannot be
relied on to prevent such a catastrophe. In a period of tension
and crisis, the danger of miscalculation or accident would
be aggravated by the shortness of missile warning times,
which give no chance for negotiation. Either nation, con-
vinced that the other was planning an attack, might seek the
advantage of striking first. Any distinction between "defense"
and "offense," or between "deterrence" and "provocation,"
would vanish in practice. It is also an unrealistic hope that
limited engagements can be confined to conventional arms
or even "tactical" nuclear weapons, for the losing side would
be tempted to turn to more powerful weapons. Such risks are
increasing now that several smaller nations have both the
capacity and the determination to produce atomic bombs.
Moreover, there is a major moral dilemma here. Many people
who assume that the possession of nuclear missiles will prevent their use also believe that the Christian conscience cannot sanction the actual employment of such methods of mass
annihilation. Yet deterrence requires the willingness to use

them. As a result we become callous about the evil to which we consent, assuming that the greater the terror of destructive power the less likely its use, and yet implicitly approving such destruction without limit.

Thus the most crucial issue today is controlled disarmament, which is the only defense possible against missiles. International monitoring of test suspension would be a significant first step. A ban on explosions in air, water, and space is already enforceable. On underground tests, Russia has made a major concession to submit to veto-free on-site inspection, though fear of espionage has made her hesitant to accept the frequency of inspections we demand. Perhaps the U.S. should accept inspection of a random sampling of borderline seismograph tremors; this would entail the risk that evasions might occasionally escape detection, but the value of such small tests would not be great, and the dangers in our present policy are considerable.[15] It has been suggested (e.g., by the Democratic Advisory Council) that since the AEC and the Defense Department are not interested in test suspension, we should have a National Peace Agency to conduct research on improvement of monitoring devices, as well as research for a bold Technical Assistance program. Present efforts toward disarmament are certainly infinitesimal compared to the resources and imagination devoted to the arms race.

More urgent is the establishment, even for a trial period, of an international inspection agency, which could both apply and improve detection methods, and allay some of the fears about inspection in both nations. Placing arms control machinery in the hands of the United Nations would at the same time be a step in strengthening the latter. The U.N. can also grow through the evolution of the powers it already has. Eventually a permanent police force and the pooling of sovereignty in certain areas are necessary if enforceable international law is to arise. But the important issue now is to take the first step, and a tremendous effort in this direction is justified by the stakes involved in avoiding thermonuclear war.

Another major policy issue related to science is technical assistance to underdeveloped countries. The rebellion against hunger, poverty, and disease is a revolutionary ferment around the world, the desperate discontent of the disinherited awakening to new hopes and new national awareness. Our foreign policy during the last decade has been built around the negative aim of opposition to Russia, and has failed to take positive leadership in a world-wide attack on hunger and disease. Concern for the misery of human beings demands planning for massive reconciliation instead of massive retaliation. Even our own self-interest requires such action, which would not be "foreign" aid but aid to the shrinking world of which we are an inseparable part. Interdependence in trade and in the conditions of peace requires constructive economic development in areas of rapid social change if chaos and violence are to be avoided. Communism has a great appeal to the victims of poverty, offering an explanation of what is going on, and a political blueprint for emancipation from misery. Its combination of goal and working plan, together with the example of Soviet industrialization in a generation, lures those who have never known what freedom means.

Two Massachusetts Institute of Technology economists have drawn up a detailed technical assistance plan, of which they say:

> In its essence our proposal calls for a sustained effort by the U.S. to associate its purposes and efforts with those of the aspiring new nations. Quite aside from its virtue as a means of protecting national interest, this associa-

tion could have profound and wholesome effects on the quality of our domestic life. . . . From the revolutionary beginnings of our history, the U.S. has, on balance, acted in loyalty to the conception that its society has a meaning and a purpose which transcend the nation.[16]

Such an undertaking would be costly. The total U.N. Technical Assistance budget for 1958 was $32 million (the U.S. share was 8¢ per person!); our own Technical Co-operation budget was $150 million. The sort of program for which the world crisis calls should be greater by a factor of ten; the National Council of Churches has recommended $3 billion per year for economic development abroad. If these figures loom large, recall that our military expenditures are greater by still another factor of ten (defense budget for 1960 is $41 billion). Scientists would of course have a major role in this venture. In 1958, U.N. Technical Assistance used 2,717 experts in 90 countries. A "World Development Authority" would use many more, working with local scientists. Government and universities could co-operate in training men for such work, including study of foreign languages and cultures. We have three military academies; why not a foreign service academy for diplomatic and technical personnel?

There are several scientific fields which might be emphasized in an active technical assistance program. The U.S. could take stronger initiative in the global development of nuclear power; we are regarded as the creators of atomic energy, but so far military uses have been more impressive than peaceful ones. Nuclear power will be important for areas deficient in conventional fuels; one freight car of uranium per year can supply as much energy as 4 million freight cars of coal, or one car every 8 seconds day and night. Relatively little research has been done on devices for utilizing solar energy. There are other problems raised by the fact that the world's population is now increasing by 49 million each year; new agricultural methods and sources of food must be developed, and methods of population planning employed. (Meanwhile, in a starving world we pay a billion dollars a year just to store our surplus food!) In addition, regional planning would allow the co-ordinated development of natural resources, water power, agriculture, and industry, in relation to social and economic factors; for example, a TVA-type program has been proposed for the Middle East. In all these activities it would be advantageous to operate through the U.N., with multilateral financing and international teams of experts. For the first time in history, man knows enough that no one need be hungry. It is the opportunity of the last half of the twentieth century to establish patterns through which the revolutionary force of science can meet this challenge in ways that do not sacrifice human dignity and freedom.

In regard to the domestic scene, it is the author's belief that the direction and emphasis of scientific development can be a matter of national policy without subjecting research to regimentation or political repression. It is a real threat to democracy if one of the most powerful social influences is felt to have a momentum of its own beyond human control, or if determination of the goals of science is surrendered to industry and defense. (Perhaps we need a federal Department of Science, with full Cabinet rank.) Consider the allocation of funds: 95 per cent of all research money now goes to applied research; [17] of government funds, 87 per cent goes to physical, 11 per cent to biological, and 2 per cent to social sciences. In terms of scientific policy these figures seem to reflect a disproportionate emphasis on applied work and on the physical sciences, to the neglect of pure research and biology, as well as of the social fields whose growth is essential if technology is to contribute to human welfare.

With the magnitude of human need in the world today, can one justify the extent to which applied research is directed toward what can only be called luxury items? Is color-TV really a top priority? What about our costly space programs? The motivation for subsidizing them is primarily military advantage (which has been questioned by many of those involved) [18] and pride in technical achievement (which could be sought in other accomplishments). Space research is only to a small extent governed by scientific curiosity, and even less by human need, though it undoubtedly offers considerable glamour and fascination. Even in terms of scientific gains, it is easy to lose a sense of proportion when one deals with the gigantic sums common in defense contracts. For example, a proposal has been drawn up for a series of satellite experiments to obtain the ultraviolet spectrum of light from the sun, which would be valuable astronomical data. The cost of the experiments? $35 million, or more than all research expenditures on astronomy in the whole of our history.[19]

Looking to the future, new possibilities in many fields offer amazing promise. In medicine, victory over all the major diseases appears not too distant, and the replacement of organs, including diseased hearts, has been predicted. In industry, the growth of automation will bring increases in productivity. Nuclear technology is in its infancy. Controlled hydrogen fusion may have much greater impact than peaceful atomic fission; for uranium is scarce and expensive, whereas hydrogen is literally as abundant as the ocean. Better understanding of photosynthesis is likely to yield novel methods of producing foods. The irrigation of the world's deserts to make them habitable lands is no longer an idle dream. Even weather control is not as incredible as it sounds, for there is a delicate energy balance which can be changed by thin films on lakes and ice fields, or by air-borne particles.

But with future advances, new temptations and problems will also arise. "Brainwashing" and subliminal advertising give us a hint of what psychology may do; the tranquilizers provide a sample of the power of drugs, and lobotomy a glimpse of the use of surgery to change personality. Bernal says that "genetics furnishes us with another quite independent means of modifying life through selective breeding and by the creation of mutations"; if individuals could be fashioned to specifications, who is to decide the formula for prefabricated man? Automation will also produce distinctive social and personal problems. A system in which machines tend machines will be as revolutionary as the former change in which men first tended machines. Among the major problems will be the disposal of radioactive waste; this has already created serious difficulties, with no satisfactory solution in sight.

So the years ahead will present us with decisions even more momentous than those of the past. Used creatively to fulfill the lives of persons, technology may help bring in an age of universal well-being; in an inadequate social context it may contribute to human degradation and enslavement, if not destruction or extinction. "I have set before you life and death ... therefore choose life" (Deuteronomy 30:19).

Chapter 6

THE SCIENTIST AS A PERSON

How does a scientist react to the temptations and successes of his job? Does technical training and activity tend to undermine religious faith? Although the roles of a man "as a scientist" and "as a person" are never really separable, it is illuminating to examine more closely an individual's personal response to his professional life. It was suggested at the outset that in addition to the call to serve human need, to seek truth, and to work for a better society, every Christian is called to worship God. The influence of scientific work, first on his personal life, and then on his beliefs, will be considered as a final aspect of the meaning of vocation.

A. The Pressures of the Job

Every job has its characteristic difficulties and frustrations. In scientific work, routines can be monotonous and uninspiring. There are also the disappointments of fruitless research, blind alleys followed, promising theories disproven, or apparatus abandoned. The co-ordinator of the federal cancer program refers to it as "the most challenging but the most frustrating area of research today." How many physicists have spent hair-tearing hours trying to track down trouble in an electronic circuit! "Lab neurosis" from discouragement at getting nowhere can be a vicious circle in investigations dependent on new ideas and initiative. Occasionally there is the major blow of finding that a result, in which one invested much time and effort, has already been accomplished by someone else.

Competing claims for time always face the scientist. Technical projects can easily absorb all one's time and energy. For limited periods this may be inevitable; many a graduate student has been "married to his apparatus" for several years, and when a man is hot on the trail of a promising lead he is rightly engrossed in his experiment. For some scientists, continuing absorption in the laboratory may be a sign of total dedication to their work; for others it may be in part an escape from impoverished human relationships or a drab and meaningless everyday life. For his total life pattern each individual must decide for himself how to apportion his time among the relative claims of job, community, and family. A teacher also has to reconcile the demands of the classroom with time for the research which contributes both to his own interest and status as a scientist and to his creativity as a teacher. In reading even within his own field it is all one can do to keep up on publications in the small area in which he is working—quite apart from reading on other subjects.

Personal relationships on the job may be another source of difficulty. In teaching, the boss is a high school principal, university dean, or department head. Interdepartmental rivalries, campus politics, professional jealousy, and personal friction can be serious. Every department is a power-structure easily subject to factionalism and individual ambitions. In industry, a scientist is part of the company, and co-operation and teamwork are essential. But the individual can be so subordinated to the group that he becomes the "organization man," [1] especially when pressures to conformity extend to non-scientific areas. Trying to get a pay raise or promotion involves commending himself to his employer both personally and as a scientist.

Ambition to succeed and the desire for recognition and prestige take distinctive forms in the life of the scientist.

1. *Cultural symbols of success.* America evaluates achievement largely by a man's income and what it procures (home, car, clothes, and style of life, such as that associated with "suburbia"). Another symbol of accomplishment is rank or title (e.g., Assistant Professor, Research Associate). Public prestige may take various forms. In the popular image the scientist may be thought of as somewhat odd, but he is highly respected; in a study of the public's evaluation of 90 different occupations,[2] 4 out of the 12 top job ratings were forms of scientific work, including medicine. It is gratifying to see one's name in print in a magazine or newspaper; the faces of half a dozen scientists have graced the cover of *Time* in the last year.

2. *Scientific publication.* Undoubtedly the factor that means most to a scientist is the opinion of his colleagues. In research, reputation depends largely on written reports. Advancement in most universities depends less on teaching ability than on what a man publishes.[3] Writing for professional journals is of great value, of course, because only experts in the same field are able to judge a man's contribution and benefit from it. But overemphasis on publication can lead to a stream of superficial articles and neglect of other criteria of evaluation; preoccupation with prestige in the wider professional community can displace concern for service in one's local situation.

3. *Recognition by other scientists.* There are a number of additional honors which indicate respect by colleagues, such

as election to offices in national societies and prizes for
achievement, supreme among which is the Nobel prize. Certain universities and laboratories are highly esteemed, and
from these a man considers it an honor to be offered a job.
Invitation to give a paper or major address at a professional
meeting is another tribute. People attend such meetings to
hear papers and exchange ideas, and also to meet people and
keep up personal contacts. In addition to a formal interview
system, affectionately known as the "Slave Market," there is
a more informal process of inquiry, word-of-mouth recom-
mendation, and "jockeying for position" among those seeking or offering jobs. Relationships between scientists may re-
veal a mixture of personal friendship, interest in one another's
work, and individual ambitions and insecurities. A man may
spend most of the convention with a former crony with whom
he feels secure, or station himself near the exit to say hello to
anyone he knows, or seek out new acquaintances. What will
he talk about, and at what points will his professional interests
and ambitions enter? These meetings reflect many dimensions
of the life of the scientist.

In addition to its distinctive frustrations and symbols of
success, the job of the scientist also has its own peculiar
temptations. "Professional ethics" are not as explicitly defined
as in some occupations because they are for the most part
inherent in the nature of the enterprise or are enforced by the
operations of the scientific community itself. But cases of
fraud dot the history of research. A Viennese zoologist proved
that the acquired characters of the spotted salamander could
be inherited, until it was discovered that the "spots" had been
applied with ink. Piltdown man, discovered in 1911, was
widely accepted by paleontologists; in 1953, fluorine tests and
X-ray spectrographs showed that a modern ape's jawbone had

been skillfully disguised to match a human upper skull. Scores of papers describing the curious properties of N-rays appeared in French journals, and the French Academy awarded its prize to their discoverer; N-rays were later shown to be imaginary.[4]

Temptations to dishonesty experienced by most research specialists are more subtle and easier to rationalize. In the race for priority, results are sometimes published with inadequate data. It is usually legitimate to mention only experiments that worked and to neglect results that seem inconsistent, but occasionally one is tempted to report only the data that support a hypothesis. Failure to give due credit is another dubious way of enhancing one's reputation. A serious violation would be the use, without acknowledgment, of someone else's ideas or preliminary results given in conversation. There is also a delicate balance as to the relative credit to be given among members of a group responsible for a project. Some department chairmen and laboratory directors have a reputation for publishing papers with their own names appearing first, when all the ideas and all the work were those of other professors or graduate students.

Some of the rationalizations which might occur in applied science were mentioned in an earlier chapter. Unethical goals may be set by one's employer; scientists have been party to production of useless "patent medicines" or even harmful drugs. Mild forms of deception or exploitation of the public are more common, as when spurious scientific claims are made for a product. Again, the experience of wielding power can be a heady one. In the last few years those in high positions in industrial laboratories and government agencies have had considerable control over the lives of other men. When scientists move in the company of senators, generals, and corporation executives, all the temptations to use power in

the service of personal ambition are present, and can easily
be disguised behind the pretext that decisions are "purely
technical."

In presenting the frustrations, ambitions, and temptations
of work in science, we have not been trying to paint a pessimistic picture. The difficulties do not preclude finding great
satisfaction in this work; 87 per cent of 4,000 scientists sur-
veyed answered "Yes" to the question "If you had it to do
over again, would you choose the same line of study?" [5] Nor
do they succumb extensively to temptations, at least in their
grosser forms. Yet any realistic account should recognize these
problems of human frailty arising in the personal dimension
of the job, rather than portray the common idealized version
of the life of the scientist. The Christian faith has significant
resources to contribute to a man's reaction to such pressures.

Consider, for example, the question of professional ambition. It would be impossible to draw any sharp line between
legitimate hope of recognition and undue preoccupation with
personal prestige. "Careerism" and "getting ahead" in reputation are not as absent as one might think from high-sound-
ing speeches about "the scientist's single-minded dedication
to truth." One wonders how many papers would be published
if all journal articles had to appear anonymously! Christianity
has always been realistic about the subtlety of ambition, and
sensitive to the dangers when it becomes a dominating motive. But there is also a legitimate place for satisfaction in a
job well done, or for the pride of the craftsman in his work.
Reacting against the doctrine that pride is always the essence
of sin, and influenced by the findings of psychiatry concerning
the opposite danger of excessive self-depreciation, a number
of contemporary theologians have pointed to the need for
self-respect. Here is the basis for a balanced view of the desire to succeed and acceptance of the fact that a superior piece

of work should be acknowledged. A person's reactions to the progress of his work will also be influenced by his religious outlook. Crushing defeat by frustrations and failures on the one hand, or arrogance in the experience of success on the other, will be less devastating if he does not see his scientific work as the only source of meaning and value in his life. He can be less preoccupied with his reputation if it is not the object of his ultimate concern.

Moreover, religious faith which is central in an individual's life affects his relationships to other persons. In interaction with colleagues, with the boss, or with other scientists, these interpersonal factors are always present. When we are insecure, we are self-centered and anxious about our own status and the impression we are making. But the person who knows the security of acceptance by God can be less apprehensive about his status in the eyes of others, less compelled to defend his own ego. He can be sensitive to the needs of those around him, concerned about the quality of human relationships, and alert for opportunities to encourage reconciliation where there is tension. Having known God's love in his own life, he can perhaps in gratitude mediate something of that love to others.

Christianity is also relevant to the temptations of the job. It does not bring any simple moralistic "Christian answer" or an absolute set of rules to be followed. Christian ethics as we have presented it consists rather in the individual's response to God and the neighbor in each concrete situation. Choices are usually not black and white, but ethically ambiguous; yet our understanding of the nature of God does influence our reactions, and gives us a basis for decision beyond personal gain or reputation. In response to God and man, each individual must decide how to divide his time, how to use his power, and how to channel his work toward constructive ends.

B. The Influence of Science on Beliefs

What effect does the scientist's training and work have on his beliefs? One hazard which arises in any specialized field is the tendency to identify a partial perspective with the whole of existence. The biologist studies man as a biochemical mechanism, and it is easy for him to go on to say: man is *just* a biochemical mechanism. *Reductionism* is the interpretation of higher levels of organization exclusively in terms of lower levels, e.g., "Psychology is just biology, biology is essentially chemistry; atoms alone are real." We have already noted Galileo's distinction between "primary qualities" (mass and extension) and the "secondary qualities" which he believed to be subjective sensations produced by the particles constituting the actual world. Whitehead has called this "the fallacy of misplaced concreteness," the tendency to attribute concrete existence only to one particular set of abstractions, or to use one type of analysis to the exclusion of other modes of description.

The reductionistic approach appears inadequate on several grounds. Laplace claimed that he could predict all future events from knowledge of the position and velocity of every particle. But the future behavior of atoms is unpredictable; and even if we did know their positions and velocities, it is dubious whether we would know everything about the events involved. Not all kinds of experience are describable in terms of such variables. The extreme view that a person is "just a collection of atoms" is less persuasive in the light of tracer studies showing that the atoms in our bodies are replaced every few years; [6] the self that continues must be constituted by the relationships and patterns among atoms, rather than by the atoms in themselves. Today it is easier to uphold the validity of various levels of explanation, related to each other and yet each having distinctive concepts and categories. Behavior is analyzed in terms of a total pattern and not simply as an aggregate of parts. The concept of organism seems to be a more fundamental image of nature than the machine. There is thus a greater willingness to grant ontological status to factors occurring in higher levels of life and in human existence.

Somewhat broader than reductionism, and hence more alluring to many scientists, is the philosophy of *naturalism,* one variation of which holds: "Only that with which science deals is real." This viewpoint is a live option today, but must be defended as a philosophical interpretation and not as a conclusion of science. For it was suggested earlier that the methods of the sciences are selective, deliberately concentrating on certain aspects of experience. If this is true, one cannot decide on the basis of science alone whether the scientific description of existence can be complete. The point is delightfully illustrated in Eddington's parable about the zoologist studying deep-sea life by means of a net of ropes on a two-inch mesh. After repeated expeditions he concluded that there are no fish smaller than two inches in the sea! So also in scientific work certain types of variables are selected from the wide spectrum of experience. Von Weizsäcker puts it this way: "The physical view of the world is wrong, not in what it asserts, but in what it omits." [7] If a naturalistic criterion is presupposed in the definition of "evidence," all else is dismissed as illusory. The biology teacher who says, "I'll believe in the soul when I see one in the laboratory" shows his presupposition that only the visible should be taken seriously. Conversation between adherents of naturalism and theism is basically an argument not between science and theology, but between two ultimate commitments, two metaphysical interpretations of the nature of the universe and the significance of human life.

"Scientism" is a term sometimes used to refer to a dog-

matic belief in the unlimited applicability of the methods of science. Others have called this "methodological imperialism," because it attempts to impose on all fields the methods which have been found successful in the natural sciences. This view ignores the limitations of science, e.g., its selective and abstractive character and its inability to deal with a unique event (see Chapter 4). Scientific understanding aims at a particular type of knowledge, namely, reproducible relations expressible in general laws. It is interested in individual events or objects only as repeatable instances of general laws.

Consider by contrast what a history teacher means when he says he wants to help his students understand an event, say the French Revolution. His primary interest is not the formulation of universal laws, but the analysis of a unique pattern among various occurrences and personalities. We might call this goal "configurational understanding," the attempt to see how the parts of an unrepeatable whole are related to each other. General theories, though they may emerge, are not the primary concern here. So also confrontation by a work of art, music, or literature is primarily a question of insight into the relations among its parts. Even the clinical psychologist, though interested in general laws, seeks to discern relationships between aspects of the particular client whom he is counseling. The theologian might add that for each person the basic religious questions deal with the significance of his individual life—the only one each of us experiences from the inside—and his relation to the singular God, who is never one of a general class of objects. In all of these areas understanding of a "configurational" rather than a scientific sort is called for.

There is one further limitation overlooked by those who preach the omnicompetence of science. The scientific enterprise is *detached and objective,* and cannot deal with personal involvement. To be sure, the scientist as a person is very much involved in his work. He has strong individual motivations; human qualities such as creative imagination and personal judgment are essential, as Polanyi has pointed out.[8] But only limited aspects of the scientist's personality are directly related to the work itself. Moreover, he deals with the public world as his object of investigation, and observational techniques are objectively standardized. Public verification is sought, which means results repeatable by other competent observers, or "intersubjective testability" within the scientific community. The so-called "involvement of the observer" in modern physics refers not to the observer as a person but to the effects of the measuring process on the results, which might even be recorded by an automatic camera. So the data reported in "public science" are strictly impersonal.

It is an amazing process of refinement by which the exceedingly human activity that goes on in the laboratory—broken test tubes, bright ideas, discussions with colleagues—ends up as a single sentence in a journal: "The reaction was found to be aided by the addition of 3% NaOH." We try to impress this impersonality on our students in the very wording of reports. The English Department might be delighted to receive a theme reading: "I took the block, and though I had a headache, I put it on the scales. . . ." But for us it must be written impersonally: "The block weighed. . . ." H. D. Smyth puts it vividly: "We have a paradox in the method of science. The research man may often think and work like an artist, but he has to talk like a bookkeeper in terms of facts, figures, and logical sequences of thought." [9] Thus the results of research are public, objective, and impersonal.

In contrast, *personal involvement* is necessary in many areas of life. In the social sciences the observer cannot stand entirely outside the social and historical process he is studying, and in the humanities the attitude of the detached spec-

tator yields only limited understanding. Participation and response are the essence of art and literature. The deepest
knowledge of another individual requires involvement in a
relationship of trust and love. Again, though the sciences can
investigate significantly many aspects of human behavior, the
full meaning of human selfhood can never be discovered ex-
ternally. Total participation rather than detached speculation
is also a prerequisite of relationship to the biblical God who
acts primarily in the sphere of personal existence. The inability of science to deal with personal involvement consti-
tutes a limitation often overlooked by proponents of "scientism."

We must then allow a place in our picture of the universe
for categories not reducible to those of science, and must preserve a role among the functions of the mind for other methods than those of the scientist. The analysis and synthesis of
the philosopher, the imagination and insight of the poet and
artist, the experience of the prophet and the mystic—these
involve distinctive categories, distinctive methods, and distinctive languages of communication. The thoughtful scientist
will want to be aware of the influence of reductionism, naturalism, and "scientism" on his own thinking. A careful cri-
tique of philosophical views claiming to be scientific is also
his responsibility as an interpreter of science.

C. The Religious Faith of the Scientist

The scientist's attitudes may also have a more direct impact
on his religious faith. Some men have reported a strong negative influence, occasionally even the loss of appreciation of all
areas outside their field of specialization. Charles Darwin
wrote: "Disbelief crept over me until at last it was so complete ... that higher tastes were gradually atrophied in the
process. . . . I could not endure to read a line of poetry, and

could derive little pleasure from a fine landscape." [10] Such extremes are rare; enjoyment of art and music is in fact rather common among scientists. Earlier a survey was cited indicating that 70 per cent of scientists say they believe in the existence of God. E. L. Long has made a study of the writings of American scientists on the subject of religion [11] and finds that they have much the same spectrum of religious beliefs as the populace at large, ranging from nontheistic outlooks (P. W. Bridgman, P. Frank) and views of God as cosmic structure or first cause (A. Einstein, A. H. Compton, R. A. Millikan) to Christian theism (K. F. Mather, W. L. Poteat, H. S. Taylor) and biblical conservatism (American Scientific Affiliation). Long concludes that science alone cannot determine a life philosophy, and that many of these authors overestimated the extent of its influence on their beliefs.

Science may not be the determinative factor in religious faith, either pro or con, but it has some valuable contributions to make. The critical study of religion has been largely the product of the scientific spirit in the West. Archeological evidence and literary analysis have helped us understand what biblical authors were saying in the context of their times, giving us a clearer picture of their developing religious insights. In the study of world religions the ideas of other faiths have been encountered. Science also helped liberate man from superstitious and magical views of religion. Again, arguments from order and design in nature may be an inadequate basis for a living relationship to God, but they still have a significant role. Modern knowledge of the universe is a warning against an anthropomorphic image of God; any conception we have must be worthy of the atom and the galaxy. Theology, like science, grows and changes; it must not isolate itself from the new understanding of the world and of man.

Moreover, similarities in method between science and religion should be noted, as well as the differences to which we have been pointing. Both areas involve two basic factors: *experience* and *interpretation*. In science these are called observation and theory. We have seen that scientific concepts are interpretive constructs, products of man's mind as it seeks to organize and correlate experience. Experience in the case of religion includes man's response of reverence, his sense of dependence and finitude, his moral experience and prayer. The writers of the Bible were not speculating in the abstract; they were trying to understand and interpret what had happened in their lives. Note also the central role of the community in both cases—the scientific community on the one hand, and the religious community or church on the other. Each community has its own symbolic language in terms of which it interprets experience, and these symbols have little meaning for the outsider in either case. In practical operation, both use language as if it were a literal description of reality, and only in more reflective moments is this symbolic and interpretive character recognized.

Furthermore, the ethical attitudes implicit in science are valuable in religion. As we outlined these, they included rationality, honesty, universalism, co-operation, freedom, and open-mindedness. The last of these requires further analysis. How is *open-mindedness* to be reconciled with the personal involvement and commitment necessary in religion? Suspended judgment is preferable to naïve credulity, and openness toward new ideas should never be lost. But the scientist may be unduly tentative if he seeks a degree of certainty that is not possible in deciding one's philosophy of life. The degree of conclusiveness of theistic belief should be compared, not with that of science, but with that of naturalism, for no philosophy can be "proved." Because of his training, the scientist may be very hesitant to commit himself. Trying to pin some people down to a definite position on any subject is like trying to nail jello to the wall. But the decisions of life force us to take positions and to act and live in terms of some faith, whether we like it or not. What passes for suspended judgment is often in effect a decision for agnosticism or naturalism. The choice is not whether to have faith or not to have it; the only choice is: *faith in what?* What is a man's ultimate allegiance; on what does he actually rely?

The religious life of the scientist should thus include a balance, and perhaps an alternation, between *personal involvement* and *reflective detachment*. Personal involvement, we have said, is needed to understand many areas of life: art, literature, knowledge of another person, and experience of God. Such commitment does not turn probabilities into certainties, but it does take one beyond a purely theoretical view of life. In Protestant thought, faith does not mean acceptance of certain infallible propositions on the authority of the church, but refers to an attitude of personal trust, self-giving, and willingness to act. If one is too detached, he may cut himself off from the very sorts of experience that are most crucial in understanding religion; but on the other hand if one becomes too uncritically involved, he may lose the capacity for reflection and evaluation. Commitment alone without inquiry can become narrow dogmatism; whereas inquiry alone without commitment ends in skepticism and detachment from real life.

There are also particular sorts of religious commitment which encourage freedom of inquiry. The prophets of all ages have denied that religion is automatically a good thing, and have usually reserved their keenest criticism for the practices of their own religious community. The Protestant Principle, as Tillich conceives it, stresses self-criticism, and rejects any human institution, creed, or theology as final. The interpretation of religious experience must be continually re-evaluated and tested in the process of living. Paul wrote: "Test everything; hold fast what is good" (1 Thessalonians 5:21). This process of experiential testing is not altogether unlike the empirical component of science, though here the laboratory is the individual's life. Our beliefs must reflect the most adequate, consistent, and comprehensive interpretation of all human experience.

Such an over-all perspective on life is always organized around a few crucial events, ideas, and categories of interpretation. A nation, for example, interprets its present experience in terms of key events in its past; the United States sees the meaning of its life today in the light of the Declaration of Independence. For the Christian community, the life of Christ is such a key event which illuminates the rest of life and helps us to understand ourselves and what has happened to us. This is Richard Niebuhr's definition of *revelation:*

> Revelation means for us that part of our inner history which illuminates the rest of it and which is itself intelligible. Sometimes when we read a difficult book, seeking to follow a complicated argument, we come across a luminous sentence from which we can go forward and backward and so attain some understanding of the whole. Revelation is like that. . . . The special occasion to which we appeal in the Christian church is called Jesus Christ. . . . Revelation means this intelligible event which makes all other events intelligible.[12]

The person of Christ is not something we could have deduced from general rational principles; he is a given event in history. But we can know the power of that event to help us understand moral choice, personal relationships, and our corporate experience as a church. Men and women through the ages have also spoken of a reorientation of one's life in which, at least partially, anxiety and internal conflict can be replaced by an inner unity and sense of direction; self-defensiveness and pretense by the ability to look at oneself honestly; self-centeredness and alienation from other people by a new capacity for genuine concern; and guilt and insecurity by a sense of God's forgiveness and acceptance.

Critical evaluation of one's religious beliefs requires theological literacy. It is no easy task for the scientist, whose education may have been narrowly specialized and whose hours are crowded, to achieve some familiarity with the best current religious thought. Excellent paperbacks and new books in religion,[13] scholarships at summer seminars, and discussion groups in churches and on campuses make this essential task easier. Responsibility with respect to one's own religious life is also crucial. If beliefs and experience interact, the impoverishment of the latter inevitably harms the former. And despite the continuing emphasis in this volume on the necessity of serving God in daily work, worship and prayer remain central expressions of the Christian's response to God. These must be the basis of continued growth in understanding the meaning of the Christian faith, in finding God's power in one's life, and in that self-commitment in action from which intellectual debates can be an escape. For the scientist, as for anyone else, the place to begin is with himself.

Finally, the man with two loyalties—to science and to religion—should have thought about the interrelations between these areas at the theoretical as well as at the practical level. One word for describing their relationship is "complementary." The aspects of reality which the sciences select for study are, in general, those about whose detailed structures religion has nothing to say. In this view the historical "conflicts" have been due to failure to observe this distinction, when the church attempted to prescribe technical conclusions, or when scientists made unwarranted interpretive statements. In scientific research one type of variable is abstracted from the rich variety of human experience, which includes the holy, the beautiful, and the moral. The same flower or sunset may be described within diverse frames of reference by the poet or artist and the botanist or meteorologist. Even within physics, alternative categories of explanation for the same phenomenon are sometimes needed. Niels Bohr used the word "complementarity" to refer to the description of light as both wave and particle. Though these are unified in the mathematical formalism of quantum theory, varying modes of representation are still useful in varying situations.

In comparing dissimilar aspects of man's life, it may be even more desirable to use several frames of reference or modes of description if one is to avoid reductionism. Asking distinctive sets of questions, one will use distinctive types of explanatory scheme, none of which is all-inclusive. The man who says, "Love is not real because I cannot weigh it" is mixing two frames of reference; "love" is not a useful concept in the same contexts in which weighing is a useful operation. If one asks, "Why did that man climb the mountain?" the physiologist's mechanical explanation in terms of metabolic and muscular factors does not preclude the psychologist's teleological analysis of the lure of the peak. We need various types of language to express various areas of experience, for each field abstracts from the total situation those aspects in which it is interested. According to such a view, science and religion ask differing types of questions, refer to differing aspects of experience, and serve differing functions in man's life, and thus provide complementary modes of description.

The scientist with an intelligent and vital religious faith has many significant opportunities to give expression to his beliefs. As a layman he has a central role in the life of the church and of society. Too often the church's witness has been delegated to a professional leadership that was to some extent cut off from the daily life of the world. People expect a minister to speak about moral and religious values, and find it easy to discount his words; the same statement by a layman often commands respect. The prestige of the scientist in our culture gives considerable influence to whatever he does. He can use this influence responsibly, in writing or speaking outside his area of specialization, only if he takes care to inform himself about the social and theological issues involved. Some scientists have gone overseas as medical, agricultural, or scientific missionaries and teachers; are there not in America most of the same opportunities for service to mankind and for witness by word and work to one's religious faith? A person's contribution is the whole of his life, which includes his acceptance of civic responsibility, his participation in the life of the church, and his personal relationships in the community and on the job. Von Weizsäcker has asserted:

> The scientist is never only a scientist. He is at the same time a living human being, a member of mankind. And so his responsibility for the particular is counter-balanced by his share of responsibility for the whole. He has to ask himself: what is the meaning of my inquiry for the lives of my fellows? [14]

It was suggested initially that every Christian is called to serve human need, to seek truth, to work for a better society, and to worship God. There are many jobs through which this fourfold calling can be expressed, in widely varying forms. Our concern has been to examine some of the ways in which these may be embodied in the life of the man who has particular talents, interests, and training in the natural sciences. It would be disastrous if every scientist with religious concern deserted his field to enter the ministry; for these may be precisely the persons who can be most influential in redirecting a technological civilization to serve human values. The world needs scientists who both do their job well and do it with social vision. And the church needs laymen who carry the gospel into the life of the world in both deed and word.

NOTES

All scripture quotations are from the Revised Standard Version of the Bible, copyrighted 1946 and 1952 by the Division of Christian Education, National Council of Churches, and used by permission.

CHAPTER 1. *Introduction: The Vocation of the Scientist*

1. "The Scientists," *Fortune,* October, 1948, p. 106.
2. R. L. Calhoun, *God and the Day's Work* (Association Press, 1957); J. O. Nelson, ed., *Work and Vocation* (Harper, 1954).
3. *Science and Public Policy* (U.S. Government Printing Office, 1947), Vol. 3, App. 3.

CHAPTER 2. *Applied Science and Human Welfare*

1. D. L. Cohn, "Great Turning Point," *Saturday Review,* May 16, 1953, p. 10. Used by permission.
2. K. F. Mather, "The Natural Sciences and the Christian Faith," *The Christian Scholar,* June, 1953, p. 123. Used by permission.
3. W. G. Pollard, "The Place of Science in Religion," *ibid.,* p. 110.
4. "The Franck Report," published in *Minutes to Midnight* (Bulletin of the Atomic Scientists, 1950). Used by permission.
5. L. Morton, "The Decision to Use the Atomic Bomb," *Foreign Affairs,* January, 1957, p. 344. Used by permission.
6. M. Armine, *The Great Decision* (Putnam, 1959), p. 241. Copyright 1959 by Michael Armine, and used by permission.
7. J. R. Oppenheimer, "Physics in the Contemporary World," *The Technology Review,* February, 1948, edited at the Massachusetts Institute of Technology, pp. 202–203. Used by permission.
8. P. W. Bridgman, "Scientists and Social Responsibility," *Scientific Monthly,* 1947, p. 150. Used by permission.

9. E. Milner, "Why Social Irresponsibility," *SSRS Newsletter,* October, 1958, p. 3.
10. N. Wiener, "A Scientist Rebels," *Atlantic Monthly,* January, 1947, p. 46.
11. F. L. Vaughan, *The U.S. Patent System* (Univ. of Oklahoma Press, 1956), chap. 8; E. H. Sutherland, *White Collar Crime* (Dryden Press, 1949).
12. C. Grobstein, "Washington Listening Post," *Bull. At. Sci.,* January, 1954, p. 27. See also issue of May, 1953.
13. W. Pigman and E. Carmichael, "An Ethical Code for Scientists," *Science,* June 16, 1950, p. 643.
14. C. W. Hume, "Ethics of Experiments on Animals," *Nature,* February 10, 1951, p. 213.
15. The Gray Board Report, *Bull. At. Sci.,* June, 1954, pp. 248–249.
16. *The Oppenheimer Transcript* (U.S. Government Printing Office, 1954). See also C. P. Curtis, *The Oppenheimer Case* (Simon & Schuster, 1955), and *Bull. At. Sci.,* May, June, and September, 1954.
17. "Concurring Opinion of Thomas E. Murray," *Bull. At. Sci.,* September, 1954, p. 277.
18. T. White, "U.S. Science: the Troubled Quest," *The Reporter,* September 23, 1954, p. 26. Used by permission.

CHAPTER 3. *Scientific Research and the Pursuit of Truth*

1. Quoted in J. H. Hildebrand, *Science in the Making* (Columbia Univ. Press, 1957), p. 89.
2. J. Bronowski, *Science and Human Values* (Messner, 1956), chap. 1.
3. *Ibid.,* p. 90.
4. A. D. Ritchie, *Civilization, Science, and Religion* (Penguin Books, 1945), pp. 167–168. Used by permission.
5. M. Polanyi, *Science, Faith, and Society* (Oxford Univ. Press, 1946).
6. T. Parsons, *Essays in Sociological Theory* (The Free Press, 1949), chap. 8.
7. See A. Standen, *Science Is a Sacred Cow* (Dutton, 1950).
8. See A. N. Whitehead, *Science and the Modern World* (Mentor Books, 1948), chap. 1; J. Baillie, *Natural Science and the Spiritual Life* (Oxford Univ. Press, 1951).
9. W. G. Pollard, "The Place of Science in Religion," *The Christian Scholar,* June, 1953, p. 117. Used by permission.
10. C. A. Coulson, *Science and Christian Belief* (Univ. of North Carolina Press, 1955), p. 101.

11. E. Schrödinger, *What Is Life?* (Cambridge Univ. Press, 1944).
12. A. Einstein, *The World as I See It* (Covici Friede, 1934).
13. E. F. Caldin, *The Power and Limits of Science* (Chapman & Hall, 1949).
14. F. Ligle, *The Abuse of Learning* (Macmillan, 1948).

CHAPTER 4. *The Science Teacher and the Student*

1. See chapters by H. S. Taylor in H. N. Fairchild, ed., *Religious Perspectives in College Teaching* (Ronald Press, 1952); K. F. Mather in P. M. Limbert, ed., *College Teaching and Christian Values* (Association Press, 1951).
2. J. B. Conant, *On Understanding Science* (Mentor Books, 1947).
3. H. Priestley, *Introductory Physics* (Allyn and Bacon, 1958).
4. W. C. Michels and A. L. Patterson, *Elements of Modern Physics*, pp. 1–2. Copyright 1951, D. Van Nostrand Company, Inc., Princeton, N.J., and used by permission.
5. G. Holton, *Introduction to Concepts and Theories in Physical Science* (Addison Wesley, 1952).
6. J. B. Conant, ed., *Harvard Case Histories in Experimental Science* (Harvard Univ. Press, 1957).
7. H. K. Schilling, chap. 5 in A. L. Sebaly, ed., *Teacher Education and Religion* (American Association of Colleges for Teacher Education, 1959). This chapter includes an excellent bibliography.
8. See H. Margenau, *The Nature of Physical Reality* (McGraw-Hill, 1950).
9. W. C. Dampier, *A History of Science* (Cambridge Univ. Press, 4th ed., 1948), p. xxii. Used by permission.
10. E. A. Burtt, *Metaphysical Foundations of Modern Science* (Doubleday, 1954), p. 305.
11. I. G. Barbour, "Indeterminacy and Freedom: a Reappraisal," *Philosophy of Science,* January, 1955, p. 8.
12. E.g., E. McCrady in H. N. Fairchild, ed., *op. cit.;* C. E. Raven, *Natural Religion and Christian Theology* (Cambridge Univ. Press, 1953); A. F. Smethurst, *Modern Science and Christian Beliefs* (Abingdon, 1955).
13. C. A. Coulson, *Science and the Idea of God* (Cambridge Univ. Press, 1958), p. 16.
14. C. H. Waddington, *The Scientific Attitude* (Penguin Books, 1948).
15. R. B. Lindsay, "Entropy Consumption and Values in Physical Science," *American Scientist,* September, 1959, p. 378. (Italics supplied)
16. P. E. Jacob, *Changing Values in College* (Harper, 1957).

CHAPTER 5.   *Science and the Social Order*

1. W. A. Leys, "The Political Philosophy of Scientists," *Bull. At. Sci.,* January, 1951.
2. R. E. Marshak, "The Nature of the Scientific Challenge," *Bull. At. Sci.,* February, 1958, p. 85; see also issues of February, March, and August, 1952, May and December, 1957.
3. E. Shils, *The Torment of Secrecy* (The Free Press, 1956), p. 46. Used by permission.
4. M. Polanyi in E. P. Wigner, ed., *Physical Science and Human Values* (Princeton Univ. Press, 1947).
5. B. Barber, *Science and the Social Order* (The Free Press, 1952), chap. 10.
6. R. Niebuhr, *The Children of Light and the Children of Darkness* (Scribner, 1944), p. vi.
7. W. G. Pollard, "The Christian and the Atomic Crisis," *Christianity Today,* October 13, 1958.
8. Editorial in *New York Times,* October 7, 1957, p. 26–C.
9. See H. R. Niebuhr, *Christ and Culture* (Harper, 1951).
10. L. Pauling, *No More War* (Dodd, Mead, 1958); E. Teller and A. L. Latter, *Our Nuclear Future* (Criterion Books, 1958).
11. J. Schubert, "Fetal Irradiation and Fallout," *Bull. At. Sci.,* June, 1959, p. 253.
12. H. Brown, "What Is a Small Risk?" *Saturday Review,* May 25, 1957, p. 9. Used by permission.
13. Congressional Hearings of May, 1957, quoted in *Bull. At. Sci.,* January, 1958, p. 59.
14. Copyright *Punch,* London, and used by permission.
15. *Bull. At. Sci.,* March, 1959, and February, 1960.
16. M. F. Millikan and W. W. Rostow, *A Proposal: Key to an Effective Foreign Policy* (Harper, 1957), p. 149. Used by permission.
17. W. W. Whyte, *The Organization Man* (Doubleday, 1957), p. 240.
18. L. A. DuBridge, "Sense and Nonsense about Space," *Harper's Magazine,* August, 1959; S. F. Singer, "The Use and Uselessness of Outer Space," *The Reporter,* June 11, 1959.
19. E. U. Condon, private communication.

CHAPTER 6.   *The Scientist as a Person*

1. "The Organization Scientist," part V in W. W. Whyte, *The Organization Man.*
2. B. Barber, *Science and the Social Order,* p. 102.
3. T. Caplow and R. McGee, *The Academic Marketplace* (Basic Books, 1958).

4. M. Gardner, *Fads and Fallacies in the Name of Science* (Dover Publications, 1957).
5. "The Scientists," *Fortune,* October, 1948, p. 106.
6. S. Glasstone, *Sourcebook of Atomic Energy* (Van Nostrand, 1958), pp. 529 ff.
7. C. F. von Weizsäcker, *The World View of Physics* (Univ. of Chicago Press, 1952), p. 28.
8. M. Polanyi, *Personal Knowledge* (Univ. of Chicago Press, 1958).
9. H. D. Smyth, quoted in G. Holton, *Introduction to Concepts and Theories in Physical Science,* p. 236.
10. F. Darwin, *Life and Letters of Charles Darwin,* Vol. 1, pp. 100, 304.
11. E. Long, *Religious Beliefs of American Scientists* (Westminster Press, 1952).
12. H. R. Niebuhr, *The Meaning of Revelation* (Macmillan, 1941), p. 93. Used by permission.
13. W. Spurrier, *Guide to the Christian Faith* (Scribner, 1953); L. H. DeWolf, *A Theology of the Living Church* (Harper, 1953). See also the "Layman's Theological Library" series (Westminster Press); the "Christian Faith" series (Doubleday); and the "Reflection Books" series (Association Press).
14. C. F. von Weizsäcker, *History of Nature* (Univ. of Chicago Press), p. 2. Copyright 1949 by University of Chicago, and used by permission.

HADDAM HOUSE is an editorial venture in the area of religious literature, which has grown out of the common concerns of The Edward W. Hazen Foundation, the Young Men's Christian Association, and the Young Women's Christian Association. It is interested primarily in the moral and religious questions of students and other young people, although many of its books appeal to a wider audience, including the leaders and teachers of youth.

Through an Editorial Advisory Committee HADDAM HOUSE studies the changing needs for religious literature, plans books, and seeks as authors not only experienced writers but also new voices qualified to give fresh guidance to young men and women in these days. The present membership of the Editorial Advisory Committee includes: Richard T. Baker, *Chairman,* Richard C. Gilman, *Secretary,* Graham Baldwin, William G. Cole, Virginia Corwin, John D. Maguire, John O. Nelson, Prentiss L. Pemberton, James Rietmulder, Roger L. Shinn, Jean M. Whittet, Winnifred Wygal.

See the following pages for a complete list of HADDAM HOUSE books published to date.

HADDAM HOUSE BOOKS

Beyond This Darkness Roger L. Shinn
Christian Faith and My Job Alexander Miller
Primer for Protestants James Hastings Nichols
Preface to Ethical Living Robert E. Fitch
The Grand Inquisitor Fyodor Dostoevsky
Youth Asks about Religion Jack Finegan
Young Laymen—Young Church John Oliver Nelson
The Human Venture in Sex, Love, and Marriage
Peter A. Bertocci
Science and Christian Faith Edward LeRoy Long, Jr.
A Gospel for the Social Awakening Walter Rauschenbusch
The Christian in Politics Jerry Voorhis
Rediscovering the Bible Bernhard W. Anderson
Life's Meaning Henry P. Van Dusen
That All May Be One James Edward Lesslie Newbigin
The Quest for Christian Unity Robert S. Bilheimer
The Christian Student and the Church
J. Robert Nelson, Editor
The Christian Student and the University
J. Robert Nelson, Editor
The Christian Student and the World Struggle
J. Robert Nelson, Editor

127

BL 240.2 .B35

Barbour, Ian G.

Christianity and the
  scientist
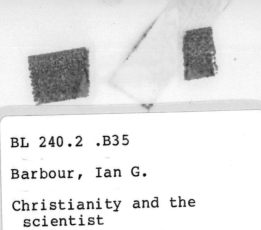